For 80 years Bais Chinuch Horav Dessler The Hebrew Academy of Cleveland

has educated, inspired and instilled emunah and bitachon essentials

while building communities and transforming generations.

Thank you for being an important part of this legacy and for joining us tonight.

HEBREW ACADEMY OF CLEVELAND

80TH SCHOLARSHIP TRIBUTE DINNER

at the Cleveland Museum of Art

March 20,2023   כ"ז אדר תשפ"ג

Great Jewish Faith

Great Jewish

Published by

ARTSCROLL®

Mesorah Publications, ltd

MORRIS J. SETTON ע"ה EDITION

Faith

A Panorama of Emunah and Bitachon Essentials by Torah Personalities

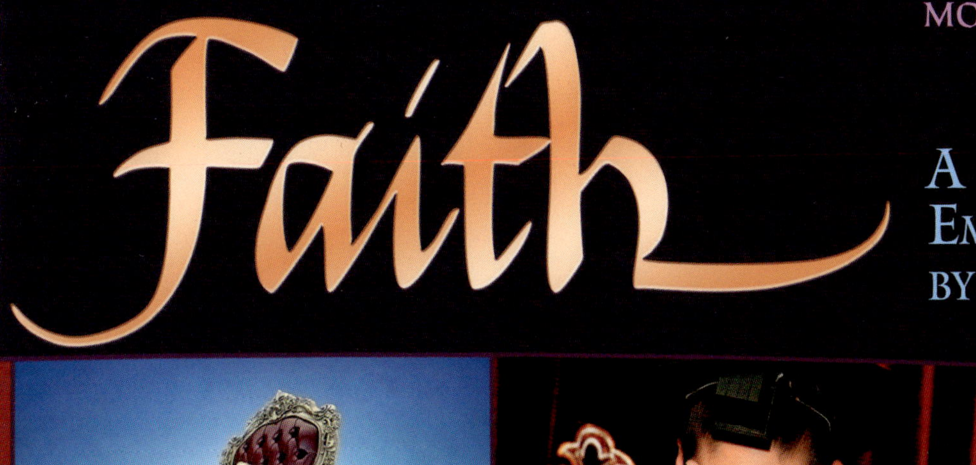

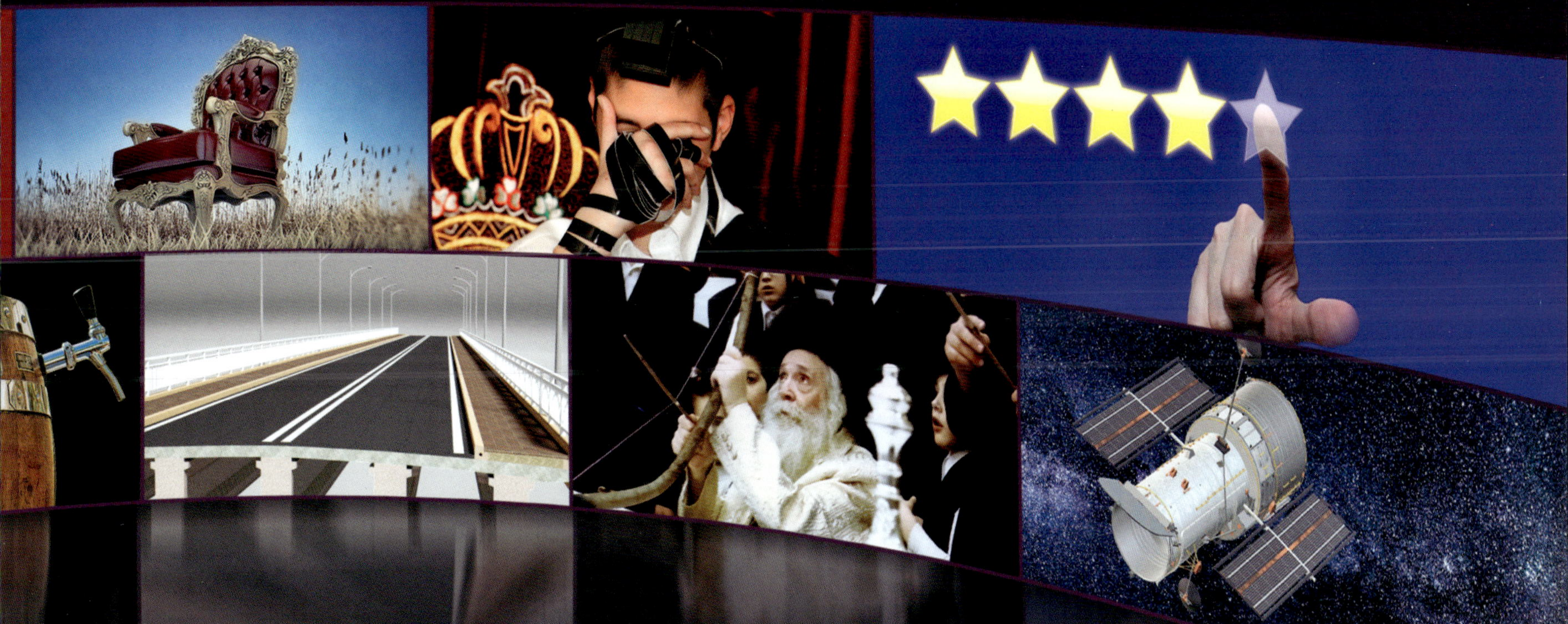

RABBI MOSHE BAMBERGER

לע"נ

צבי בן חיים יעקב ע"ה

יהודית משא בת נח ע"ה

Who imbued their family with a love of *Yiddishkeit*.
Their integrity was inspirational.
What they did for each other, their family, and their
fellow Jew remains forever.

In memory of

NORMA STEINBERG ע״ה

Nechama bas Moshe Gershon HaCohen

By Mr. Steve and Dr. Alissa Grill

In honor of

RABBI MOSHE BAMBERGER

This book should be a source of emunah
for all those searching for their *zivug*.

Meir Simcha

Dedicated by Dr. Isaac Madeb and Family
לע״נ

LILY LEAH MADEB BAT VIRGINIA ע״ה

לע״נ

BREINDEL BAS EPHRAIM FISCHEL ע״ה

1 אֲנִי מַאֲמִין I believe with complete faith that the Creator, Blessed is His Name, creates and guides all creatures, and that He alone made, makes, and will make everything.

2 אֲנִי מַאֲמִין I believe with complete faith that the Creator, Blessed is His Name, is unique and there is no uniqueness like His in any way, and that He alone is our God, Who was, Who is, and Who always will be.

3 אֲנִי מַאֲמִין I believe with complete faith that the Creator, Blessed is His Name, is not physical and is not affected by physical phenomena, and that there is no comparison whatsoever to Him.

4 אֲנִי מַאֲמִין I believe with complete faith that the Creator, Blessed is His Name, is the very first and the very last.

5 אֲנִי מַאֲמִין I believe with complete faith that the Creator, Blessed is His Name — to Him alone is it proper to pray and it is not proper to pray to any other.

6 אֲנִי מַאֲמִין I believe with complete faith that all the words of the prophets are true.

7 אֲנִי מַאֲמִין I believe with complete faith that the prophecy of Moshe our teacher, peace be upon him, was true, and that he was the father of the prophets — both those who preceded him and those who followed him.

8 אֲנִי מַאֲמִין I believe with complete faith that the entire Torah now in our hands is the same one that was given to Moshe our teacher, peace be upon him.

9 אֲנִי מַאֲמִין I believe with complete faith that this Torah will not be exchanged nor will there be another Torah from the Creator, Blessed is His Name.

10 אֲנִי מַאֲמִין I believe with complete faith that the Creator, Blessed is His Name, knows all the deeds of human beings and their thoughts, as it is said, "He fashions their hearts all together, He comprehends all their deeds."

11 אֲנִי מַאֲמִין I believe with complete faith that the Creator, Blessed is His Name, rewards with good those who observe His commandments, and punishes those who violate His commandments.

12 אֲנִי מַאֲמִין I believe with complete faith in the coming of the Messiah, and even though he may delay, nevertheless I anticipate every day that he will come.

13 אֲנִי מַאֲמִין I believe with complete faith that there will be a revivification of the dead whenever the desire emanates from the Creator, Blessed is His Name and exalted is His mention, forever and for all eternity.

א אֲנִי מַאֲמִין בֶּאֱמוּנָה שְׁלֵמָה, שֶׁהַבּוֹרֵא יִתְבָּרַךְ שְׁמוֹ הוּא בּוֹרֵא וּמַנְהִיג לְכָל הַבְּרוּאִים, וְהוּא לְבַדּוֹ עָשָׂה וְעוֹשֶׂה וְיַעֲשֶׂה לְכָל הַמַּעֲשִׂים.

ב אֲנִי מַאֲמִין בֶּאֱמוּנָה שְׁלֵמָה, שֶׁהַבּוֹרֵא יִתְבָּרַךְ שְׁמוֹ הוּא יָחִיד וְאֵין יְחִידוּת כָּמוֹהוּ בְּשׁוּם פָּנִים, וְהוּא לְבַדּוֹ אֱלֹהֵינוּ, הָיָה הֹוֶה וְיִהְיֶה.

ג אֲנִי מַאֲמִין בֶּאֱמוּנָה שְׁלֵמָה, שֶׁהַבּוֹרֵא יִתְבָּרַךְ שְׁמוֹ אֵינוֹ גוּף, וְלֹא יַשִּׂיגוּהוּ מַשִּׂיגֵי הַגּוּף, וְאֵין לוֹ שׁוּם דִּמְיוֹן כְּלָל.

ד אֲנִי מַאֲמִין בֶּאֱמוּנָה שְׁלֵמָה, שֶׁהַבּוֹרֵא יִתְבָּרַךְ שְׁמוֹ הוּא רִאשׁוֹן וְהוּא אַחֲרוֹן.

ה אֲנִי מַאֲמִין בֶּאֱמוּנָה שְׁלֵמָה, שֶׁהַבּוֹרֵא יִתְבָּרַךְ שְׁמוֹ לוֹ לְבַדּוֹ רָאוּי לְהִתְפַּלֵּל, וְאֵין לְזוּלָתוֹ רָאוּי לְהִתְפַּלֵּל.

ו אֲנִי מַאֲמִין בֶּאֱמוּנָה שְׁלֵמָה, שֶׁכָּל דִּבְרֵי נְבִיאִים אֱמֶת.

ז אֲנִי מַאֲמִין בֶּאֱמוּנָה שְׁלֵמָה, שֶׁנְּבוּאַת מֹשֶׁה רַבֵּנוּ עָלָיו הַשָּׁלוֹם הָיְתָה אֲמִתִּית, וְשֶׁהוּא הָיָה אָב לַנְּבִיאִים, לַקּוֹדְמִים לְפָנָיו וְלַבָּאִים אַחֲרָיו.

ח אֲנִי מַאֲמִין בֶּאֱמוּנָה שְׁלֵמָה, שֶׁכָּל הַתּוֹרָה הַמְּצוּיָה עַתָּה בְּיָדֵינוּ הִיא הַנְּתוּנָה לְמֹשֶׁה רַבֵּנוּ עָלָיו הַשָּׁלוֹם.

ט אֲנִי מַאֲמִין בֶּאֱמוּנָה שְׁלֵמָה, שֶׁזֹּאת הַתּוֹרָה לֹא תְהֵא מֻחְלֶפֶת וְלֹא תְהֵא תּוֹרָה אַחֶרֶת מֵאֵת הַבּוֹרֵא יִתְבָּרַךְ שְׁמוֹ.

י אֲנִי מַאֲמִין בֶּאֱמוּנָה שְׁלֵמָה, שֶׁהַבּוֹרֵא יִתְבָּרַךְ שְׁמוֹ יוֹדֵעַ כָּל מַעֲשֵׂה בְּנֵי אָדָם וְכָל מַחְשְׁבוֹתָם, שֶׁנֶּאֱמַר: הַיֹּצֵר יַחַד לִבָּם, הַמֵּבִין אֶל כָּל מַעֲשֵׂיהֶם.

יא אֲנִי מַאֲמִין בֶּאֱמוּנָה שְׁלֵמָה, שֶׁהַבּוֹרֵא יִתְבָּרַךְ שְׁמוֹ גּוֹמֵל טוֹב לְשׁוֹמְרֵי מִצְוֹתָיו וּמַעֲנִישׁ לְעוֹבְרֵי מִצְוֹתָיו.

יב אֲנִי מַאֲמִין בֶּאֱמוּנָה שְׁלֵמָה, בְּבִיאַת הַמָּשִׁיחַ וְאַף עַל פִּי שֶׁיִּתְמַהְמֵהַּ, עִם כָּל זֶה אֲחַכֶּה לּוֹ בְּכָל יוֹם שֶׁיָּבוֹא.

יג אֲנִי מַאֲמִין בֶּאֱמוּנָה שְׁלֵמָה, שֶׁתִּהְיֶה תְּחִיַּת הַמֵּתִים בְּעֵת שֶׁיַּעֲלֶה רָצוֹן מֵאֵת הַבּוֹרֵא יִתְבָּרַךְ שְׁמוֹ וְיִתְעַלֶּה זִכְרוֹ לָעַד וּלְנֵצַח נְצָחִים.

INTRODUCTION

Baruch Hashem, the *Great Jewish* series has brought out the vibrancy of our illustrious Torah personalities from a rich palette of colors: their letters, speeches, artifacts, books, photographs, and quotes.

And these volumes have made an impact.

The positive feedback comes in — from rabbis whose *derashos* have been enhanced; teachers whose classrooms have become enlivened; parents whose Shabbos tables have been uplifted; and individuals — young and old alike — who have become informed and inspired.

I am often asked, "What's next in the series?" This question prompts me to explore what theme would be most beneficial for our times.

As the world reels from pandemic and war, when it struggles with social and financial unrest, we desperately seek to anchor ourselves to something permanent, something eternal. The stress and sorrow, fear and frenzy that churns the seas of life have but one calmant: emunah in Hashem. Understanding that the Almighty has a Masterplan, realizing that He alone orchestrates everything that transpires, and knowing that He always and truly loves us, these are the most vital messages we need to hear, and to convey, in our times.

Hence, our present work turns its attention to matters of faith — essential principles from *Gedolei Yisrael* on believing and trusting in Hashem, attaining closeness to Him, and making life less stressful and more tranquil. Though many fine works have been written on these topics, the uniqueness of *this* book is in the way it animates these fundamental ideas in a vivid, dramatic, and engaging way, bringing such critical lessons to life.

One hundred powerful quotes have been selected, set upon breathtaking graphics, along with accompanying commentary. Sources are brought in the back of the book. Additionally, we have added a section in which the reader becomes the writer: a special notebook in which to chronicle episodes of Divine Providence in one's *own* life, thereby fortifying faith in Hashem in the most constructive manner — through personal experience.

When I was a young man, I traveled to London for a friend's wedding. On Shabbos, we davened in a *shtiebel* in Golders Green. The Rebbe, a very old, regal man who survived the horrors of the camps, rose to speak. The shul fell silent, straining to hear the words of the *tzaddik*. He began his *derashah* by repeating, again and again, "*Aleph-Beis, Aleph-Beis, Aleph-Beis…*" I turned to my British host, who was a regular there, for commentary. He motioned to me to wait; apparently, the Rebbe began many talks in such a manner. Then, things suddenly came into focus. Choked up, the Rebbe continued, "*Emunah — bitachon, emunah — bitachon, emunah — bitachon. The Aleph-Beis* of life is emunah and bitachon…"

Such a simple, straightforward message had a profound impact on me. Authentic and alive, simple and stunning, it resonated deeply. Decades later, I remember the words as if they were just spoken.

It is my fervent hope that this book will likewise touch the reader, taking the timeless truths of Torah giants and animating them. If our mission will have been accomplished, the reader should be ushered into the happy, serene, and spiritually connected world of emunah and bitachon.

I warmly welcome feedback from my readers. For all questions, comments, or ways you were impacted by the series, I can be reached at greatjewishmail@gmail.com.

ACKNOWLEDGMENTS

I humbly offer my absolute gratitude to *Hashem Yisbarach*, Who has bestowed upon me and my family bountiful blessing and constant kindness. Working on this book has afforded me a fuller awareness of the infinite *chessed*, endless concern, and unconditional love that Hashem has for His people. It is my hope and prayer that this work brings us ever closer to Him.

My father, R' Zvi (Bjorn) Bamberger *z"l*, was a rock of emunah and bitachon, invoking Hashem's Name at every step of life. He would continually remind me, "*Der Eibeshter feert de velt* — Hashem runs the world." Hearing that message from him never failed to soothe me. I hope that my father is *shepping* abundant *nachas* from his family, who, over a decade after his passing, miss him so dearly.

My mother, Mrs. Carol Bamberger, is a woman who lives her life with such firm, unshakable trust in Hashem that it is palpable. She has also added immensely to the quality of this manuscript through her skillful editing. May she continue to enjoy her adoring children and grandchildren *ad meah v'esrim shanah*, in joy and good health.

My wife's parents, Mr. and Mrs. Martin Tropper, have always shown a unique care and concern for my family, and have taken pride in our accomplishments. I pray that Hashem grants them many years of health and happiness.

I am privileged to serve as the Mashgiach Ruchani of Beis Medrash L'Talmud/ Lander College for Men. For over two decades, we have been *zocheh* to develop genuine and wonderful *bnei Torah*. Much of the content of these books has originated from my *shiurim*, honed by the inquisitive minds and pure hearts of my *talmidim*. I am indebted to HaRav Doniel Lander, Rosh Yeshivah of Ohr HaChaim, for entrusting me with such an important role.

ArtScroll/Mesorah has surpassed even their own exceedingly high standards through the production of the *Great Jewish* series. Who could have imagined when I presented the idea of *Great Jewish Letters* to Rabbi Meir Zlotowitz *z"l* so many years ago that it would flourish into a series of this scope and reach. My dear friend Rabbi Gedaliah Zlotowitz continues to steer the ArtScroll ship with great skill, vision, and passion, as Rabbi Nosson Scherman and Rabbi Sheah Brander utilize their immense talents to glorify the *D'var Hashem.* Rabbi Scherman has carefully reviewed the content; R' Mendy Hertzberg seamlessly coordinated all the details of this project; and R' Eli Krohn designed the cover with his brilliant flair. Mrs. Esther Feierstein edited the manuscript with precision, while my superb graphic artist, Mrs. Raizy Czitter, has produced yet another work of art.

I wish to extend my heartfelt gratitude to my *yedid ne'eman*, R' Dovid Ribner (Get The Picture, 917-853-8435), for providing many of the magnificent portraits of *Gedolei Yisrael* that adorn this series. Rabbi Nochum Kaplan, R' Tzvi Friedman, R' Moshe D. Yarmish, Rachel Cohen, and Esti Hess have graciously permitted me the use of several beautiful renditions of their *Gedolim* portraits and photographs.

I greatly appreciate Rabbi David Sutton's review of the manuscript, and Rabbi Shaya Thau's patience in ensuring that the wording of certain texts were completely accurate.

I would like to publicly acknowledge some of the patrons of this work who have, with their generous spirits, enabled this book to be published: The Setton Family, Mr. Ronnie Adjmi, Mr. Steve and Dr. Alissa Grill, Dr. Isaac Madeb, and Dr. Meir Panish. Rabbi Maimon Elbaz was extremely gracious in his assistance.

I fondly remember my dear *talmid* and friend, Mr. Barry Gavarin, Baruch Ben Yosef *z"l,* who was taken from us in the prime of his remarkable life. He was a man who possessed deep faith, a passion for mitzvos, and a genuine love of Torah, *talmidei chachamim,* and family. A generous dedicator of two books in this series, his name will always be a part of this project.

Finally, to my *eishes chayil*, Risa, who is a true partner in all that I do. Her steadfast encouragement and wise guidance allow my ambitions to materialize, including the production of these books. May we continue to have boundless *nachas* from our beautiful children, Shlomo Zalman, Chava, Frieda, Golda, and Yitzchak Dov. We hope and pray that emunah and bitachon permeate their lives.

MOSHE BAMBERGER

New York 5783

"HASHEM HAS ALWAYS PROVIDED
FOR ME UNTIL TODAY.
WHY WOULD HE STOP NOW?"

— THE CHOFETZ CHAIM

We constantly worry about our livelihood, plagued by so many doubts. Will I be able to earn enough to provide for my family? Are my skills going to be marketable in the future? Will customers continue to patronize my establishment? The saintly Chofetz Chaim, **RABBI YISRAEL MEIR KAGAN** (1838-1933), imparted that we must learn to shore up our trust in Hashem, to banish such qualms from our heart. Instead of focusing on the uncertain future, look to the past. Has not Hashem always provided for my needs? The years I have been alive, with Hashem's help, have I ever missed a day without food, clothing, and shelter? Why would our loving Father in Heaven not continue to provide for me going forward?

"I HAVE TAKEN REVENGE AGAINST HITLER, YM"S. HE SOUGHT TO ELIMINATE THE JEWISH PEOPLE FROM THE FACE OF THE EARTH, AND I HAVE REBUILT A NEW GENERATION WHO CONTINUE THE LEGACY OF OUR HOLY ANCESTORS..."

— THE KLAUSENBERGER REBBE

The Rebbe at his Lag B'Omer *tish*. Photo Credit: Leibel Karmel

CONSTRUCTIVE

RABBI YEKUSIEL YEHUDAH HALBERSTAM
(1905-1994), Rebbe of the Sanz-Klausenberg
Chassidim, lost his wife, eleven children and
most of his followers during the Churban of
Europe, while himself enduring unspeakable
horrors in several concentration camps.
After the war, the Rebbe restored Jewish
communal life in the D.P camps of Western
Europe, remarried and had more children, re-
established his dynasty in the United States
and Israel, and founded an excellent hospital
in Netanya that strictly adheres to halachah.
At the wedding of his youngest daughter,
the Rebbe expressed with confidence that
through his prolific spiritual achievements
he has exacted revenge against the wicked
leader of our enemy.

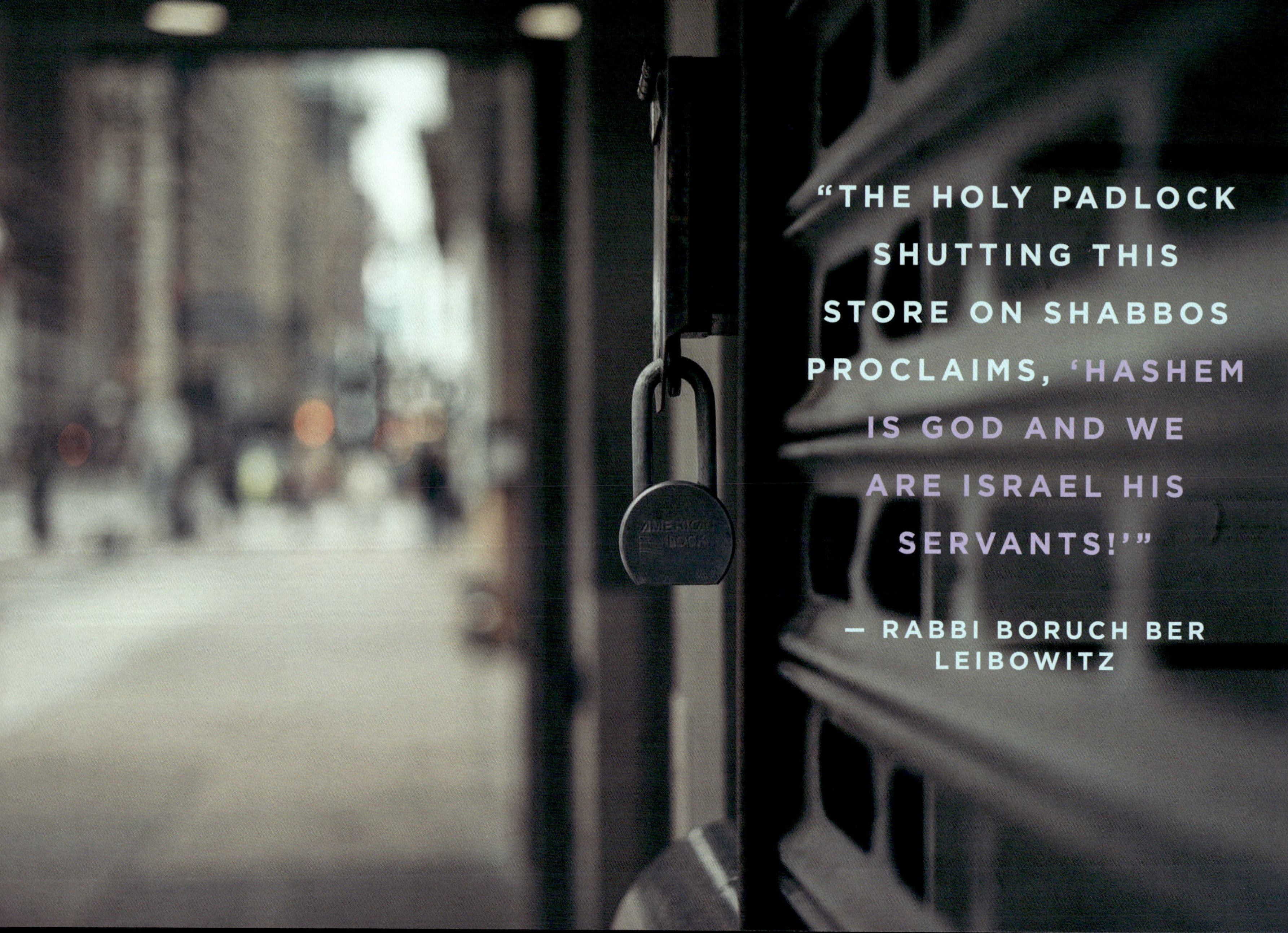

"THE HOLY PADLOCK SHUTTING THIS STORE ON SHABBOS PROCLAIMS, 'HASHEM IS GOD AND WE ARE ISRAEL HIS SERVANTS!'"
— RABBI BORUCH BER LEIBOWITZ

TESTAMENT

In 1928, **RABBI BORUCH BER LEIBOWITZ** (c. 1862-1939), eminent Rosh Yeshivah of Kaminetz, made a historic visit to the United States. He delivered encouragement to the American Jews who faced many spiritual challenges in those days, including the difficult test of not working on Shabbos. When R' Boruch Ber passed a Jewish store on Shabbos with a shut gate, he warmly kissed its padlock and declared it holy, as it attests to God's dominion and our subservience to Him. And to a Jew who approached the Rosh Yeshivah and proudly declared that he closes his store every Shabbos, R' Boruch Ber told him that if he "listens" carefully to the lock on his closed gate, it will affirm that "Hashem is the Lord!"

"IT WAS WORTH CREATING THE ENTIRE UNIVERSE AND SUSTAINING IT FOR SIX THOUSAND YEARS ALL SO THAT..."
— RABBI SIMCHA ZISSEL ZIV

Incredibly, **RABBI SIMCHA ZISSEL ZIV BROIDE** (1824-1898), the Alter of Kelm, once said, "It was worth creating the entire universe, sustaining and fueling it for six thousand years all so that — in the course of its existence — there will be at least one person who will say *Baruch Hu u'baruch Shemo* at least once in their lifetime. For this alone, the world's purpose has already been fulfilled. And yet...

- 1,000 of these *Baruch Hu u'baruch Shemos* do not measure up to the value of one *Amen*!
- 1,000 *Amens* will not measure up to the value of one *Amen yehei Shemei rabbah*!
- And 1,000 *Amen yehei Shemei rabbahs* will not add up to the value of one word of Torah!

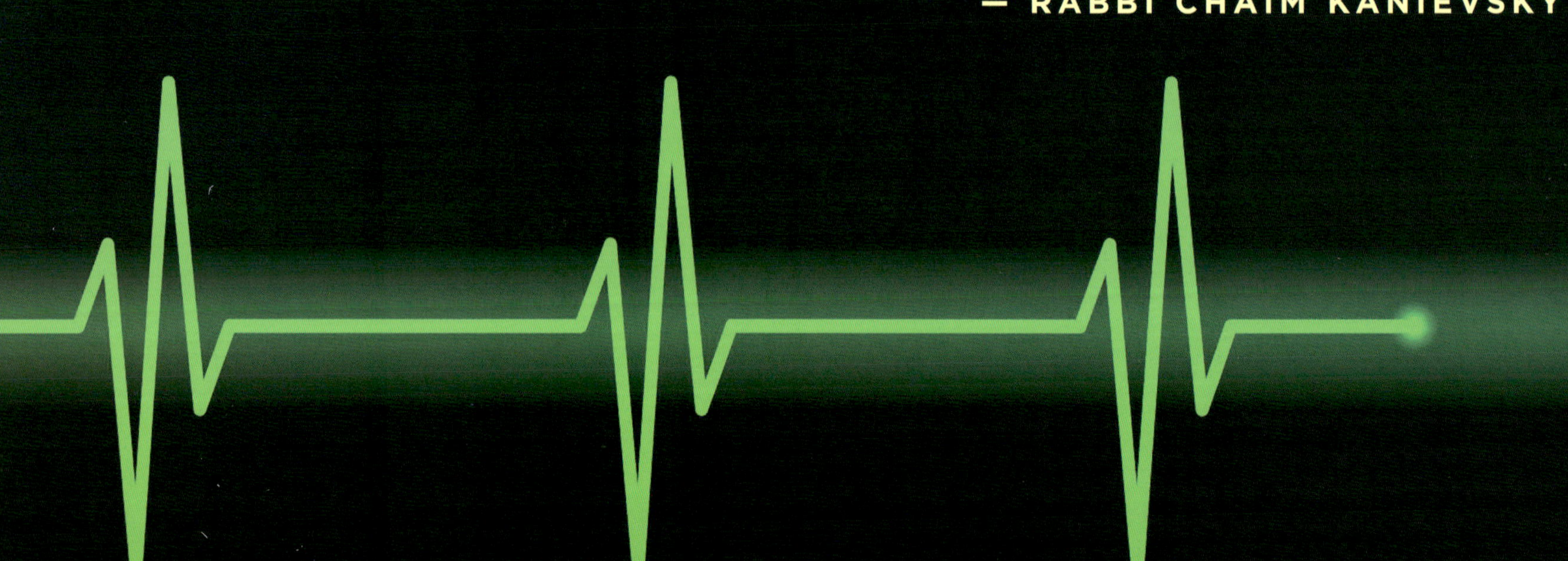
"EVERY MOMENT OF LIFE, EVEN IF ACCOMPANIED BY THE WORST SUFFERING, IS THE GREATEST GIFT A PERSON CAN HAVE."

— RABBI CHAIM KANIEVSKY

BEING

The Gemara (*Sotah* 11a) relates that Pharaoh had three advisers as to how to deal with his Jewish subjects, Bilaam, Yisro, and Iyov. Bilaam, who counseled him to enslave the Jews, was punished with death. Iyov, who kept silent, was punished with a life of pain and suffering. Yisro, who fled, was rewarded that his descendants would sit on the Sanhedrin. A question was posed to the *Sar HaTorah* (Prince of Torah), **RABBI CHAIM KANIEVSKY** (1928-2022). Why was Iyov, who remained silent, punished with a lifetime of unbearable suffering, while Bilaam, whose advice harmed the Jews, received the much quicker, relatively painless punishment of instant death? Rav Kanievsky answered that despite the torturous pain endured by Iyov all his life, he was granted the gift of life. Bilaam's life, however, was taken away — a far greater punishment. Every second of life is so valuable, for it gives one the priceless ability to serve Hashem!

"HASHEM, AT TIMES, ISSUES HARSH DECREES, BUT HE ALSO GIVES US THE STRENGTH TO WITHSTAND THEM — TO PREVAIL!"
— THE SKULENER REBBE

FORTITUDE

RABBI ELIEZER ZUSIA PORTUGAL (1898-1982), the first Skulener Rebbe, maintained his faith even in the darkest hours of WWII and imprisonment and torture under the Communists. "*Baruch gozeir u'mekayeim* — We bless God, in *Baruch She'amar*, for 'decreeing and fulfilling,'" said the Rebbe. "Are we praising God for not only issuing harsh decrees against us, but carrying them out, too?" The Rebbe suggested a new understanding of this prayer. 'He passes terrible decrees, true, but He *grants us the strength to endure* (*mekayeim*) *the worst!*" The Rebbe himself embodied this interpretation, as despite all the suffering he endured, he found Divine strength to persevere.

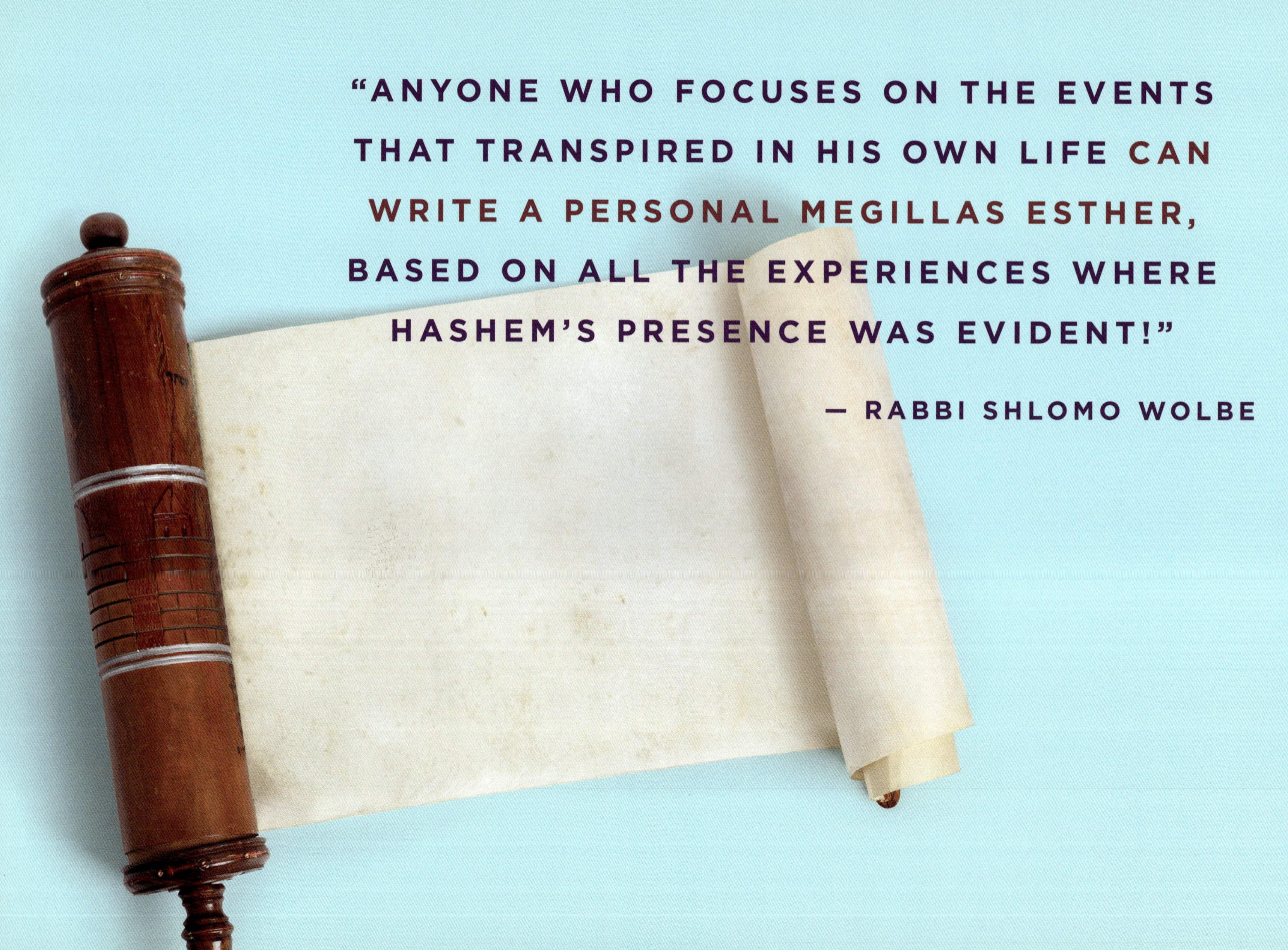

"ANYONE WHO FOCUSES ON THE EVENTS THAT TRANSPIRED IN HIS OWN LIFE CAN WRITE A PERSONAL MEGILLAS ESTHER, BASED ON ALL THE EXPERIENCES WHERE HASHEM'S PRESENCE WAS EVIDENT!"
— RABBI SHLOMO WOLBE

PROVIDENCE

One who pays attention to the events occurring to him will discover many moments that *Yad Hashem*, God's guiding hand, is unmistakable. Whether it was losing a job only to find a better one, deciding to not invest in something that ended up going out of business, or being in the "right place at the right time," one begins to see that the twists and turns of life are anything but random. **RABBI SHLOMO WOLBE** (1914-2005), profound thinker and Mussar personality, asserts that just as Megillas Esther is a chain of seemingly unrelated, non-miraculous events that — seen as a panorama — present a clear picture of Divine intervention, our lives are similar. Although God's face is hidden, He is visible to us in retrospect through His actions, prodding, guiding, and encouraging us on each step of our journey.

"YOU MEAN, YOU NEVER ONCE SAID,
'I LOVE YOU HASHEM'?"

— RABBI AVIGDOR MILLER

RABBI AVIGDOR MILLER (1908-2001) was renowned for his palpable, intense love for Hashem. He would tell others that a sure way of creating a feeling of love for God was by declaring openly, "I love You, Hashem." Simply saying those words, even if one does not yet feel it, will lead to a great outpouring of love for Him. When speaking of this topic at a family bar mitzvah, Rav Miller exclaimed, "You mean, you never once said, 'I love You, Hashem'? No? Let's all together say, 'I love You, Hashem!' I know you feel uncomfortable, but do it anyway. It's going to make a difference in your relationship."

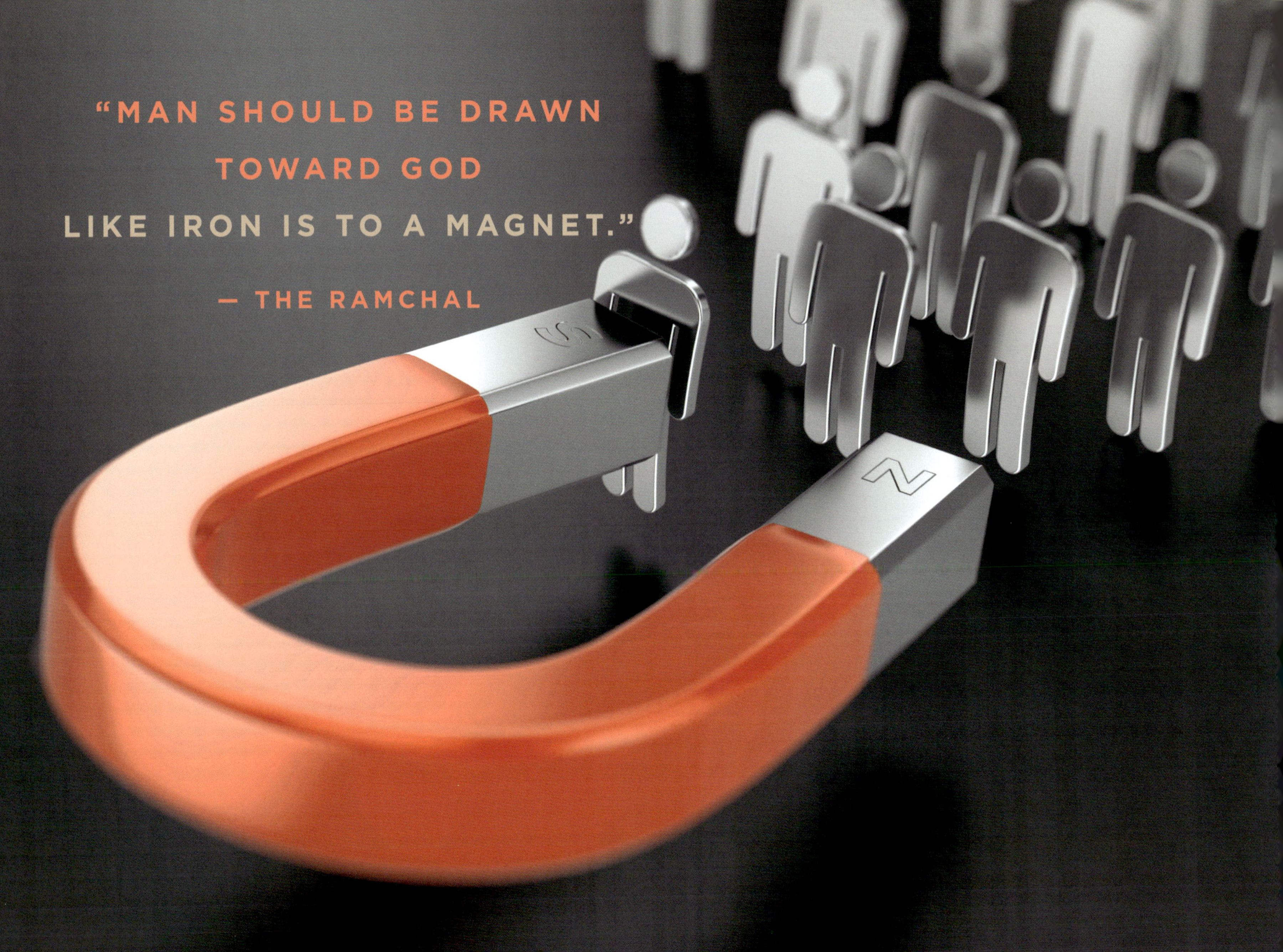

"MAN SHOULD BE DRAWN TOWARD GOD LIKE IRON IS TO A MAGNET."
— THE RAMCHAL

RABBI MOSHE CHAIM LUZZATTO (1707-1747), known by the acronym Ramchal, was an extraordinary Torah scholar and profound Kabbalist. In his Mussar classic *Mesillas Yesharim*, he describes man's purpose in this world as serving Hashem faithfully, thereby earning the supreme reward of delighting in the radiance of the Divine Presence in the Eternal World. To navigate the minefield of distractions and temptations in this world, man must orient himself solely toward God and remove all physical matters that come between Him and the Almighty, to the degree that he is drawn after Him, "As iron is drawn to a magnet." This powerful metaphor illustrates the natural attraction that our soul has for the Creator.

"AN ACT OF KINDNESS PERFORMED TODAY IS LIKE A SEED THAT BLOSSOMS FORTH SALVATION AT THE MOST BENEFICIAL TIME, EITHER FOR YOU OR FOR A FUTURE DESCENDANT."

— RABBI SAMSON RAPHAEL HIRSCH

The Torah (*Shemos* 34:7) describes Hashem as being "*Notzer chessed l'alafim* — a Preserver of deeds of kindness for thousands of generations.' **RABBI SAMSON RAPHAEL HIRSCH** (1808-1888), a leader of Ashkenazic Jewry, observes that the word "*notzer*" also means to cause to blossom. He explains that Hashem, in His benevolence, allows an act of *chessed* which we perform today to become a seed that blossoms and brings forth salvation at a later time, when it is needed most, either for ourselves or for our descendants yet unborn — even thousands of generations from now!

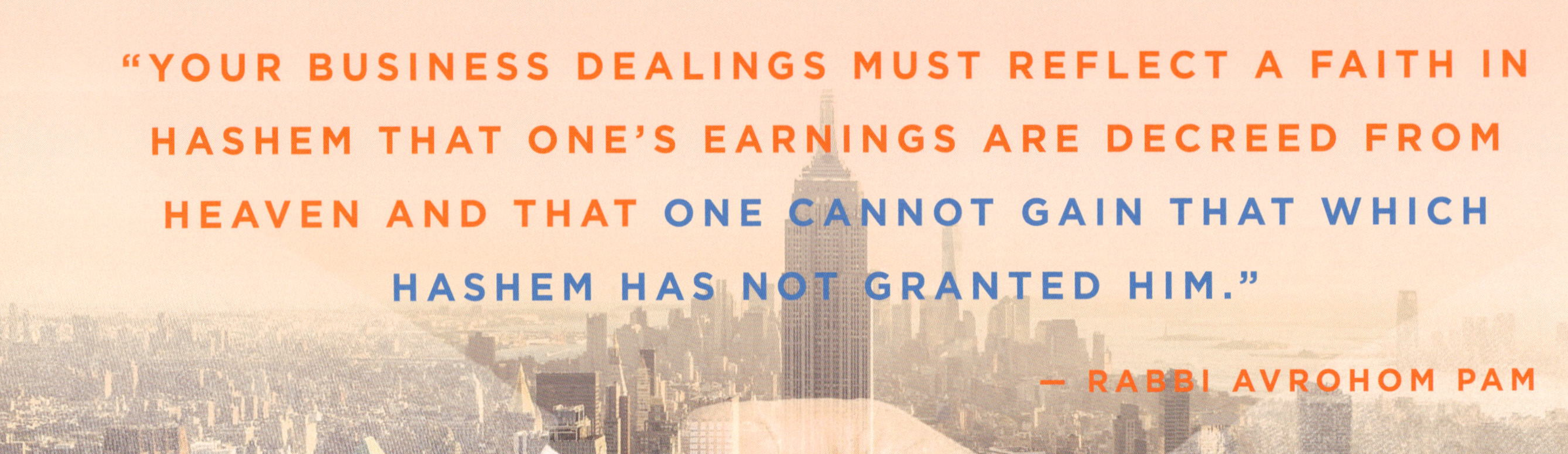
"YOUR BUSINESS DEALINGS MUST REFLECT A FAITH IN HASHEM THAT ONE'S EARNINGS ARE DECREED FROM HEAVEN AND THAT ONE CANNOT GAIN THAT WHICH HASHEM HAS NOT GRANTED HIM."
— RABBI AVROHOM PAM

INTEGRITY

One of the last and most important speeches of **RABBI AVROHOM PAM** (1913-2001), beloved Rosh Yeshivah of Torah Vodaath, was on the topic of business ethics; Rabbi Elya Svei (1924-2009) referred to it as Rav Pam's *tzavaah* (ethical will). In it, he cited the Gemara in *Shabbos* (31a) that the first question a person is asked in the Heavenly Court after departing this world is, "Did you conduct your business dealings *b'emunah*, with integrity?" The word *emunah*, noted Rav Pam, can also mean, *with faith in Hashem*. In other words, were you straightforward in business, in a way that reflects a belief that God alone manages all of one's revenue, and that dishonesty will lead to no profit?

"MAINTAIN FAITH IN GOD DURING DISTRESS; FROM THE DARKNESS WILL COME THE LIGHT."
— RABBEINU YONAH

DELIVERANCE

Rabbi Yitzchak Hutner (1906-1980), Rosh Yeshivas Rabbeinu Chaim Berlin, derived from these words of **RABBEINU YONAH** (1200-1263) that someone who merely believes that "things will be fine," has not achieved true bitachon. According to Rabbeinu Yonah, one must believe that from what seems now to be the worst scenario imaginable — will emerge the greatest salvation! Rav Hutner brought an example of this from Yosef. Thrown by his brothers into a pit, and then pulled out to be sold down to Egypt as a slave, at first glance it was tragic. In retrospect, however, Hashem was planting the seed from which Yosef's ascent would sprout, providing sustenance for his family and the world!

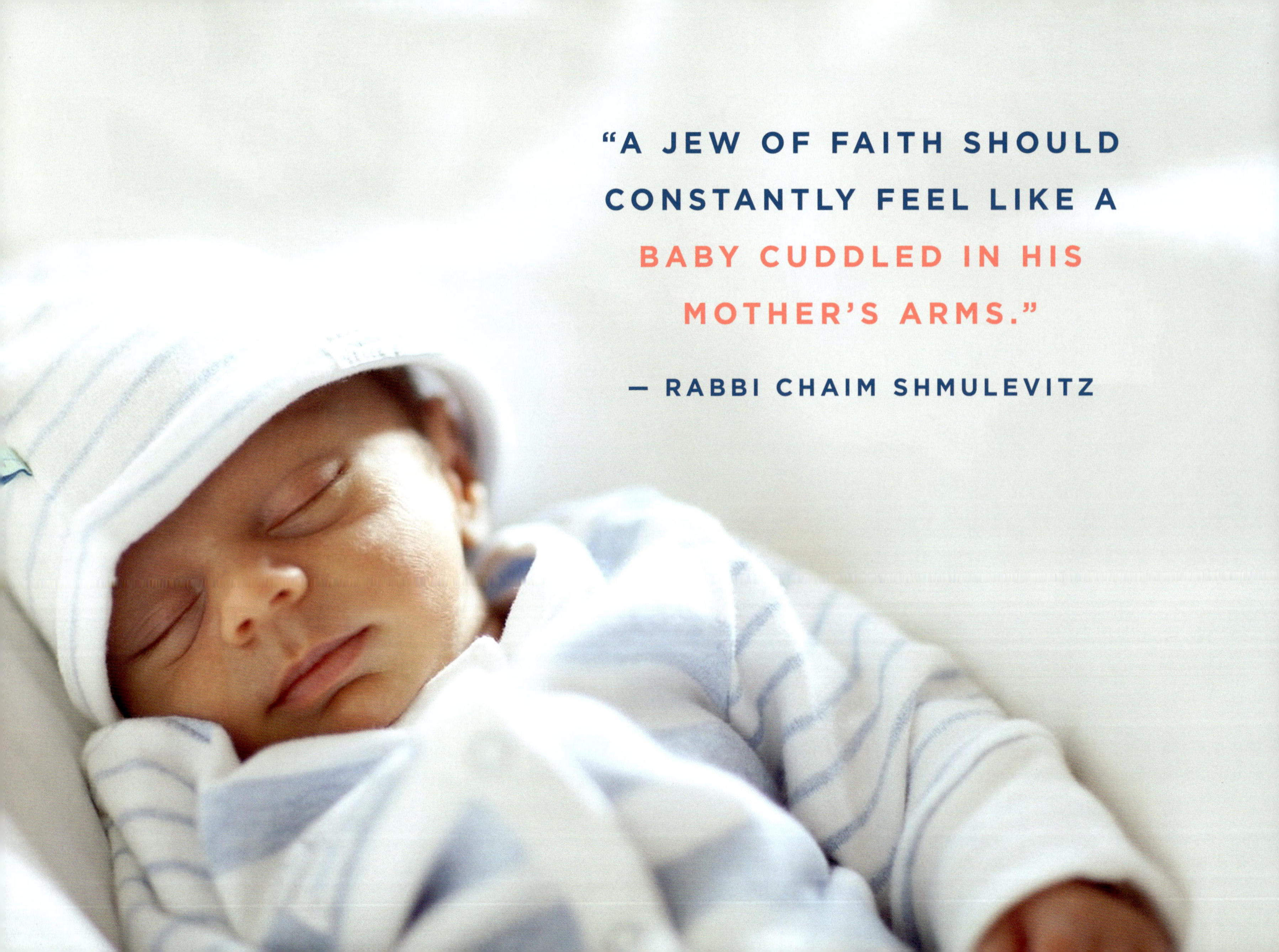
"A JEW OF FAITH SHOULD CONSTANTLY FEEL LIKE A BABY CUDDLED IN HIS MOTHER'S ARMS."
— RABBI CHAIM SHMULEVITZ

SECURE

A Jew with emunah must feel calm and secure at all times, knowing that he is in the warm, loving embrace of his Creator. The Rosh Yeshivah of Mir, **RABBI CHAIM SHMULEVITZ** (1902-1979), illustrated this with the metaphor of a baby who is nestled in his mother's arms as she travels from place to place. If the baby could communicate and you asked him, "Where are you?" he would not answer the name of the city he is in, but simply, "I am in my mother's arms." Such should be the feeling of a Jew. Regardless of what transpires throughout life's often winding, rocky road, he should feel no fear or turbulence, for he is snugly held in Hashem's arms.

"WE HAVE DONE OURS;
NOW HASHEM WILL
DO HIS."
— THE STEIPLER GAON

SUBMISSION

When certain worthy projects we have undertaken are not meeting with success, we must not become aggravated. Instead, we should take the approach that once we have done all we can, the rest is up to Hashem. The Steipler Gaon, **RABBI YAAKOV YISRAEL KANIEVSKY** (1899-1985), brought a proof to this from Avraham Avinu, who appealed to Hashem to save Sodom from destruction (*Bereishis*, ch. 18). When his plea was not accepted by God, the verse states that Avraham, "returned to his place" (ibid. v. 33). Despite the fact that his request was denied, Avraham did not become consumed by disappointment. He went on with his life's work, knowing that he did all he could. As the expression goes, "Do your best — God will do the rest."

"THE SIGN ON THE GREYHOUND BUS — 'LEAVE THE DRIVING TO US'—MAY BE APPLIED TO WHAT HASHEM SAYS TO US: 'RELAX! IT IS NOT YOUR WORLD! LEAVE THE DRIVING TO ME…'"

— RABBI SHIMON SCHWAB

CALM

RABBI SHIMON SCHWAB (1908-1995) served as the Rav of Khal Adath Jeshurun of Washington Heights, and as an eloquent spokesperson for Torah Jewry. In his last public address, on the topic of emunah and bitachon, Rav Schwab used the commercial slogan of the Greyhound Bus Company to illustrate what genuine bitachon is: realizing that whatever happens in life comes from Him, and accepting it fully. This provides a person with peace of mind, a serene feeling that he is in the best hands, unafraid of whatever life brings.

"IT IS EASY TO TRUST IN GOD WHEN LIFE IS GOOD. MUCH HARDER, THOUGH, IS MAINTAINING BITACHON WHEN ONE ACTUALLY NEEDS IT."

— THE CHAZON ISH

STEADFAST

The Torah luminary **RABBI AVRAHAM YESHAYA KARELITZ** (1878-1953), known as the Chazon Ish, wrote a *sefer* entitled *Emunah U'Bitachon*. In it, he clarifies that faith and trust in Hashem are actually the same idea, but that faith is the *theory* of relying on Hashem, while trust is putting that *into practice*. It is easy to "talk the talk" about trusting in God when things are calm and under control. Far harder is it to "walk the walk" when challenging times arise. That is the best moment to properly assess the true nature of one's theoretical trust — his emunah. Will it be practically employed, or will panic prevail and cause him to turn to ancillary means and strategies other than the Almighty to deal with the crisis at hand?

"DO NOT COVET THE POSSESSIONS OF OTHERS — HASHEM PROVIDES EVERYONE WITH EXACTLY WHAT THEY NEED TO HAVE IN LIFE."
— RABBEINU AVRAHAM IBN EZRA

The Tenth Commandment, *"Do not covet,"* is hard to understand. How can the Torah legislate against a person's desires? Isn't jealousy a natural, human response to observing others with nicer things than you? The Torah commentator, **RABBI AVRAHAM IBN EZRA** (1089-1167), explains that it is, indeed, possible to govern feelings of envy, if one would only see the possessions of others as impossibly removed from him — as "out of his league" as is a princess to a simple farmhand. Once a person has emunah that all of his belongings are what God wants him to have and all of his neighbor's possessions are what God wants his neighbor to have, he should be able to rein in any feelings of jealousy.

"FAITH IN TORAH IS CONTINGENT ON FAITH IN TORAH SAGES."
— THE CHASAM SOFE

REVERENCE

It is essential to believe that the Torah is the immutable word of Hashem. Equally critical, insists **RABBI MOSHE SOFER** (1762-1839), the illustrious Chasam Sofer, is trusting that the Torah sages throughout the ages are tasked with explaining the meaning of the Divine text. The Written Law is simply indecipherable without accompaniment of the Oral Law. Acceptance of the venerated Rabbinic leaders of each generation as the interpreters of the Torah's true intent and as issuers of rulings and decrees based on their understanding is a crucial principle upon which the entirety of the Torah rests.

"THOSE TWO SEATS ON EITHER SIDE OF THE PONEVEZH ARON KODESH ARE RESERVED FOR MASHIACH AND ELIYAHU HANAVI. THEY ARE NOT FOR SALE!"

— THE PONEVEZHER RAV

There was a family in London who offered a large donation to the Ponevezh Yeshivah, but they wanted their names to adorn the two chairs affixed to either side of the famous golden *aron kodesh* in the beis medrash. "I can't do it," the Ponevezher Rav, **RABBI YOSEF SHLOMO KAHANEMAN** (1886-1969), told them. "Those places aren't mine to sell. The family wondered who they were meant for, and the Rav told them, "One is for Mashiach and the other for Eliyahu HaNavi, and they're coming soon. Where do you think Mashiach will go first? Only to a yeshivah of course! I can't sell those chairs for all the money in the world!" Such was the intensity of emunah in Mashiach that the Rav possessed.

"FOR EVERY BREATH WE TAKE, WE OWE A COMPLETE HALLEL TO HASHEM!"
— RABBI AVRAHAM GRODZENSKY

BREATHTAKING

Life affords us so many pleasures we simply take for granted. Take, for example, the sheer satisfaction we derive when we take in and release a full breath of air! Our Sages, in fact, teach us (*Bereishis Rabbah*, ch. 14) that for every breath we must praise Hashem. **RABBI AVRAHAM GRODZENSKY** (1883-1944) takes this literally, that each time our lungs inhale and exhale we are obligated to sing a complete Hallel (not just a "Half-Hallel"!) to Hashem. Alas, we do not have sufficient time to do so, and we remain indebted to the Almighty for all those unsung praises…

My Week!  אי"ה

Sunday	Monday	Tuesday	Wednesday	Thursday	Friday	שבת

"WHEN PLANNING ANYTHING IN LIFE, STIPULATE, 'IM YIRTZEH HASHEM — PROVIDED THAT HASHEM SO WISHES.'"

— THE SHELAH HAKADOSH

INCLUSION

The Torah describes the movements of the Jewish people in the Wilderness as, "By the *mouth* of Hashem they traveled" (*Bamidbar* 9:18). The holy Shelah, **RABBI YESHAYAHU HALEVI HOROWITZ** (c. 1555-1630), finds in this verse support for the widespread Jewish custom of prefacing every move in life as it being subject to Hashem's approval. Jewish people travel through life by "the mouth of Hashem" — with lips emphasizing the critical role He plays every step of the way.

"EVEN IF A JEW SAYS MORNING, NOON AND NIGHT, 'I DO NOT BELIEVE IN HASHEM,' I FOR ONE DO NOT BELIEVE HIM!"
— RABBI ARYEH LEVINE

CORE

RABBI ARYEH LEVINE (1885-1969), the "Tzaddik of Yerushalayim," loved Jews of all stripes, seeing their inner beauty and believing in their unlimited potential. The quote comes from a letter he wrote, in which he continues, "A Jew cannot stop being a Jew, even if he has converted out of his faith. The distinctive characteristic of every Jew is that he is born with faith, having within him a spark of our father Avraham, the first of all believers. Only, with the passage of time, so much dust has gathered over that spark until it has completely covered up that faith. When troubles befall the Jews, though, they clean away the dust, and then the pure gold beneath is revealed..."

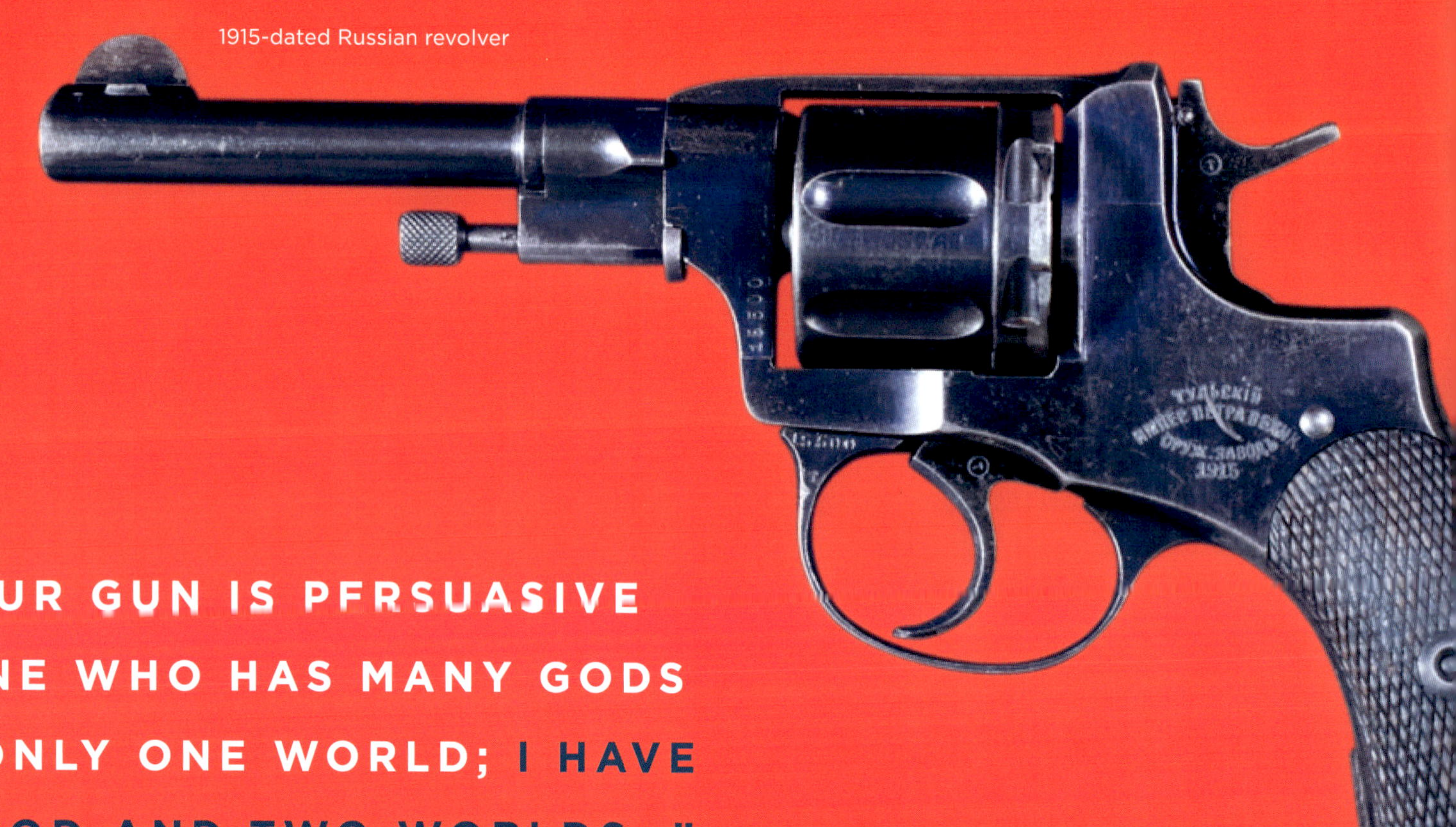

1915-dated Russian revolver

"YOUR GUN IS PERSUASIVE TO ONE WHO HAS MANY GODS AND ONLY ONE WORLD; I HAVE ONE GOD AND TWO WORLDS..."

— RABBI YOSEF YITZCHAK SCHNEERSOHN OF LUBAVITCH

COURAGE

The sixth Lubavitcher Rebbe, **RABBI YOSEF YITZCHAK SCHNEERSOHN** (1880-1950), fought a heroic battle to keep the flame of Torah Judaism alive from inside the Soviet Union. Once, a ruthless Soviet interrogator, bent on ridding the Rebbe of his religious principles, lifted the revolver that lay on the table and pointed it at the Rebbe, saying, "This 'toy' does away with 'principles.'"
"You are mistaken," replied the Rebbe. "This 'toy' impresses only the cowardly atheist, who has but a single world and many gods. But as for us, who have but a single God and believe in two worlds, the toy which you are brandishing not only fails to frighten, it makes no impression whatsoever."

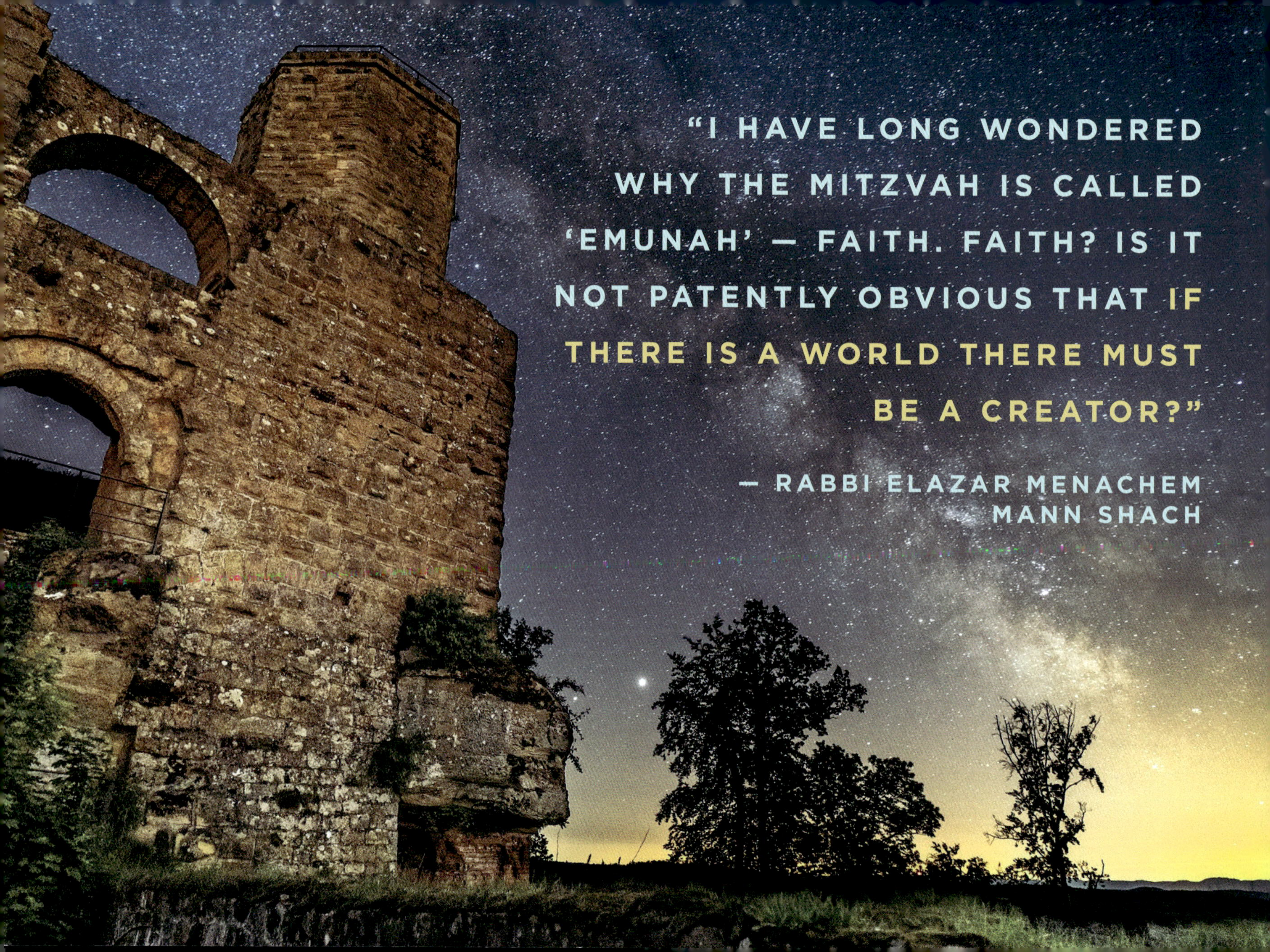

"I HAVE LONG WONDERED WHY THE MITZVAH IS CALLED 'EMUNAH' — FAITH. FAITH? IS IT NOT PATENTLY OBVIOUS THAT IF THERE IS A WORLD THERE MUST BE A CREATOR?"
— RABBI ELAZAR MENACHEM MANN SHACH

EVIDENT

This question of the Ponevezh Rosh Yeshivah, **RABBI ELAZAR MENACHEM MANN SHACH** (1899-2001), is itself a profound lesson, as it is an emphatic declaration of his absolute emunah. To Rav Shach, it was so evident that if there is a palace, there must be a builder; if there is a magnificent world, there must be a Creator. The Rosh Yeshivah writes that he asked his question to the Brisker Rav (1886-1959), who said that he, too, had the very same question, and that he had asked it of his father, Rabbi Chaim Soloveitchik (1853-1918). Rav Chaim explained that yes, to the degree that the human mind can comprehend God's greatness, the mitzvah is to *know* Hashem. The mitzvah of *faith*, however, begins where our understanding ends — beyond the scope of human comprehension.

"TO CLARIFY ONE SUBTLE POINT IN EMUNAH IS WORTH MORE THAN ANYTHING ELSE THAT I MIGHT TEACH."

— THE RAMBAM

The Rambam, **RABBEINU MOSHE BEN MAIMON** (1138-1204), was one of the greatest Torah scholars and leaders of our nation. He was also exceedingly prolific, authoring many classic *sefarim* indispensable to Torah scholarship. Still, the Rambam writes in his commentary to Mishnah (*Berachos*, ch. 9) that more than any of his extensive teachings, most dear to him is when he can elucidate a principle of faith; the most fundamental and essential of subject matters are the most imperative to convey.

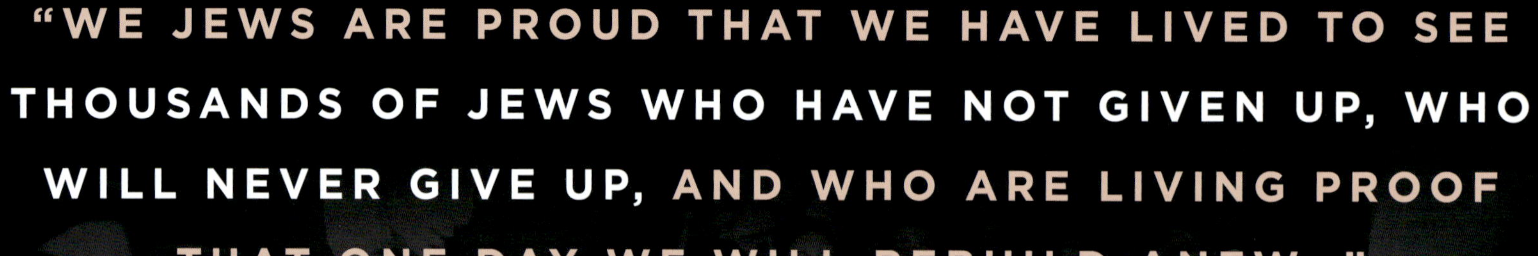

Chanukah candle-lighting ceremony in the Westerbork Transit Camp, Netherlands, 1943

PRIDE

One of the heroes of the Churban in Europe was **RABBI YISRAEL SPIRA,** the Bluzhever Rav (1889-1989), who survived the horrific nightmare of the war and continued to be a spiritual leader and inspiration to his fellow prisoners. In Bergen-Belsen, he secretly arranged, on the first night of Chanukah, to light a menorah in the presence of hundreds of Jews, who risked their lives to do so. The Rav recited the three blessings and lit the menorah. A non-believing Jew asked the Rebbe, "Rabbi Spira, I do not understand how you can bring yourself to recite the *Shehecheyanu* blessing. How can you offer thanks for having been kept alive for this time of death, torture, and hunger? We wish we were dead!" The Rebbe replied, "I, too, was wondering how I could joyfully recite these words. Then I looked around and I saw this huge assemblage of Jews that had risked their lives to participate in this mitzvah. Have you ever in your life witnessed such courage and faith? Isn't that something to be grateful for?"

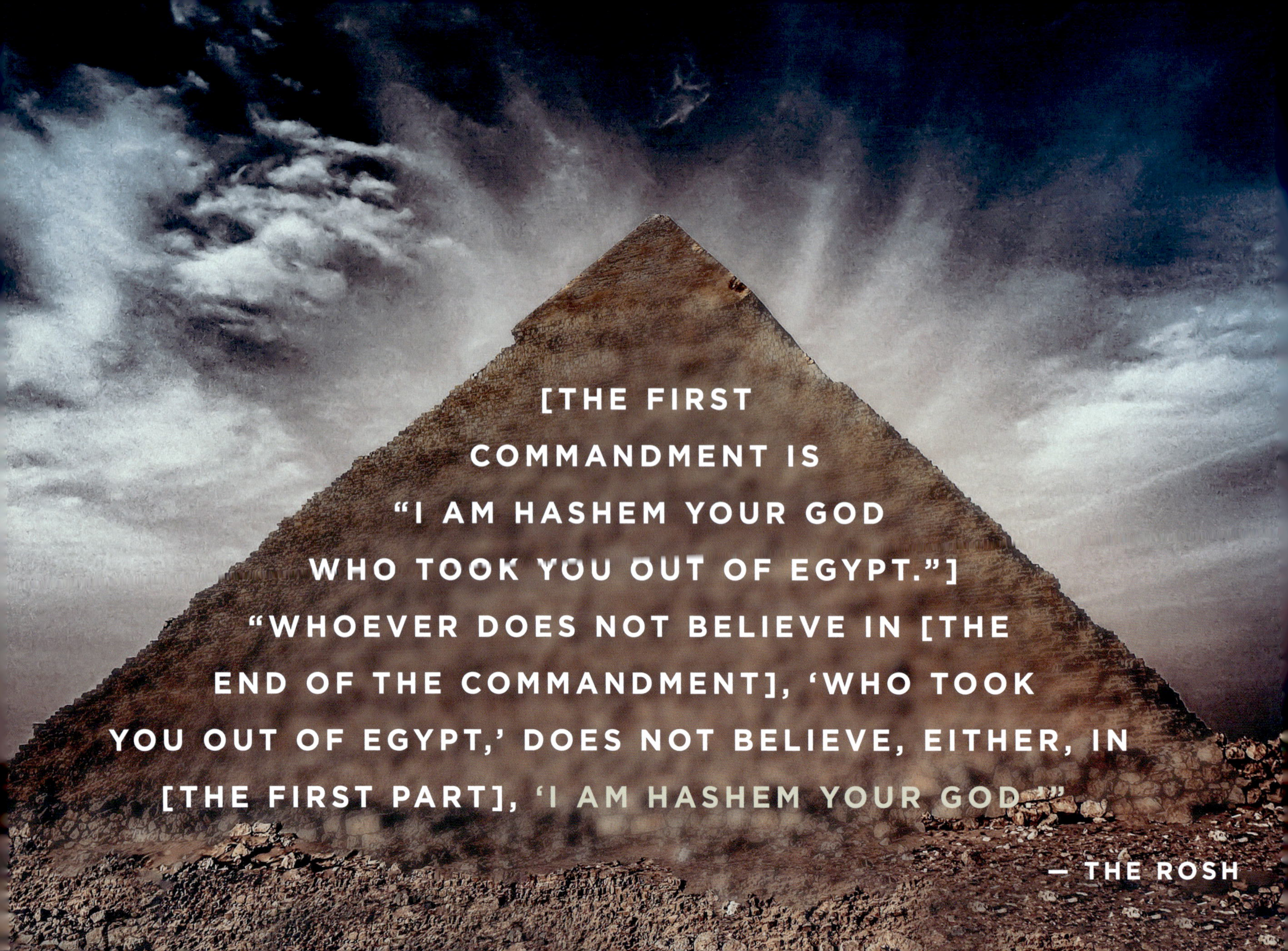
[THE FIRST
COMMANDMENT IS
"I AM HASHEM YOUR GOD
WHO TOOK YOU OUT OF EGYPT."]
"WHOEVER DOES NOT BELIEVE IN [THE
END OF THE COMMANDMENT], 'WHO TOOK
YOU OUT OF EGYPT,' DOES NOT BELIEVE, EITHER, IN
[THE FIRST PART], 'I AM HASHEM YOUR GOD.'"
— THE ROSH

INTERTWINED

The Rosh, **RABBEINU ASHER BEN YECHIEL** (1250-1327), in a passage of his ethical work, *Orchos Chaim*, speaks of the critical belief in Divine Providence (*Hashgachah Pratis*), that Hashem is constantly observing and guiding the path of every man. He insists that if one does not believe in this concept, clearly evidenced by the wonders experienced when God took us out of Egypt, this is tantamount to not believing in the existence of Hashem Himself. God and Divine intervention are interwoven; believing in one without the other is not complete faith. He concludes that this belief in Providence is what separates us from the other nations, and it is the underpinning of the entire Torah.

"DURING A SEVERE DROUGHT, WHEN ATTENDING A GATHERING TO PRAY FOR RAIN — HAVE FAITH!
BRING ALONG YOUR RAIN GEAR!"
— RABBI MOSHE GALANTI

OPTIMISM

There was a serious drought in Yerushalayim in the 17th century, and the Turkish governor, who loathed the Jews yet realized that only *their* prayers could bring rain, threatened them that if no rain fell, they would be expelled from the city. The Jews gathered in shul, fasted and cried, but the skies remained parched. **RABBI MOSHE GALANTI** (1621-1689) announced, "Everybody must gather tomorrow at the gravesite of Rabbi Shimon HaTzaddik and pray for the end of the decree; make sure to bring your raincoats and boots!" The next day, hundreds of people assembled at the gravesite, and, despite the shining sun, they wore their rain gear. After fervently praying, the heavens opened and a downpour of rain drenched the holy city for three days straight.

"AT TIMES, HASHEM SENDS US A 'KISS' TO REMIND US THAT HE LOVES US…"

— RABBI CHAIM SHMULEVITZ

The Gemara discussing Chanukah (*Shabbos* 21a) states that the festival was established because of the miracle of the single, undefiled flask of oil that was discovered by the Chashmonaim upon recapturing the Holy Temple, which miraculously burned for eight days instead of one. The Mir Rosh Yeshivah, **RABBI CHAIM SHMULEVITZ** (1902-1979), questions why this miracle was more significant than the fantastic miracle of the Chashmonaim defeating the mighty Greek army. He explains that while the military victory was an *essential* miracle, the miracle of finding the flask of oil was an *extra* miracle. It occurred for no other reason than to demonstrate Hashem's love for us, a Divine "kiss" reminding us of His enduring affection for us. This "kiss" is the basis for our beloved Chanukah... Do we ever experience those signs of love from Hashem in our own lives?

"OUR QUESTIONS EXIST ONLY IN THIS WORLD.
IN HEAVEN, ALL BECOMES CLEAR…"
— A DISCIPLE OF THE RAMBAN

The Me'am Lo'ez brings a story about the Ramban, **RABBEINU MOSHE BEN NACHMAN** (1194-1270), who visited a student who was deathly ill. Realizing that his student's time was near, the Ramban told him that there were a number of questions deeply troubling him regarding Hashem's actions in this world, specifically concerning the suffering endured by the Jewish people in that era. He asked his student that when his time comes, to please ascend to the heavens, ask these questions, and return, in a dream, with the answers. Shortly after the *talmid's* death, he appeared to his rebbe in a dream and explained that in heaven, those questions that he had prepared to ask were no longer difficult...

"WHEN WE EACH ARRIVE IN THE NEXT WORLD, WE WILL BE ASKED, 'DID YOU ANTICIPATE, WITH FULL FAITH, HASHEM'S DELIVERANCE AT EACH CHALLENGE YOU FACED THROUGHOUT LIFE?'"

— THE BEIS HALEVI

The Gemara in *Shabbos* (31a) records that one of the questions posed to us in the judgment of the Coming World is, "Did you await salvation?" While the simple understanding of this question is if we eagerly awaited the Redemption — the arrival of Mashiach, **RABBI YOSEF DOV SOLOVEITCHIK** of Brisk (1820-1892), the Beis HaLevi, expands the meaning of this question to the realm of our daily challenges of life. When faced with turmoil and uncertainty in life, did we crumble in despair, or did we await, with a heart brimming with emunah and bitachon, our personal salvation?

Rabbi Levenstein delivering a Mussar talk in Ponevezh Beis Medrash

AWARENESS

Although God's existence seems obvious, especially to advanced yeshivah students, the saintly Mashgiach of Mir and Ponevezh, **RABBI YECHEZKEL LEVENSTEIN** (1885-1974), instructed the Mussar personality Rabbi Shlomo Wolbe (1914-2005) that when he returns to his yeshivah he should bang on the *bimah* in the beis medrash and emphatically declare to his students that there is, indeed, a Creator! For some time, this directive was puzzling to Rav Wolbe, until he finally grasped the Mashgiach's instruction. True, the students spend all day learning Torah and davening, but are they always cognizant that they are learning Hashem's Torah, and that they are davening before Hashem? They must be reminded of this constantly, lest they go through the spiritual motions without being aware of *Whom* they serve.

"WHEN YOU PROCLAIM IN SHEMA THAT GOD IS THE KING OVER THE ENTIRE HEAVEN AND EARTH — DON'T FORGET TO ACCEPT GOD AS KING OVER YOURSELF, TOO."
— RABBI YISRAEL OF SALANT

CORONATION

RABBI YISRAEL LIPKIN OF SALANT (1810-1883), father of the Mussar movement, pointed out the sad truth regarding our relationship with Hashem. We are meticulous in declaring the Oneness of Hashem as King over the heavens and earth (see *Shulchan Aruch O.C.* 61:1), yet sometimes forget to accept Him as King over ourselves as well! Faith is not just believing that God created and runs the universe, but recognizing that He is our *personal* God as well, Who is deeply involved in the myriad details of our lives; in Whom we trust and on Whom we depend.

"EVERYTHING THAT EXISTS AND TRANSPIRES IN THIS WORLD IS FOR THE SAKE OF THE TORAH AND THOSE WHO STUDY IT."
— RABBI YITZCHAK ZEV SOLOVEITCHIK
Trans-Siberian Railway

PURPOSE

Rashi, at the beginning of his commentary
to the Torah, teaches us that the entire world
was created for the Torah and the Jewish
people. The Brisker Rav, **RABBI YITZCHAK
ZEV SOLOVEITCHIK** (1886-1959), gives an
example of this in modern history. The Russian
government commissioned the construction
of the massive Trans-Siberian Railway,
spanning from Moscow to Vladivostok. It was
completed in the early 1900s, at phenomenal
cost, both in terms of human life and
resources. The Divine purpose of that massive
undertaking became clear when it transported
yeshivah students — most notably the Mir
— from war-torn Europe to Japan, thereby
allowing them to miraculously escape the
clutches of death.

"ONE SHOULD CHOOSE TRUTH,
SIMPLY BECAUSE IT IS THE TRUTH."

— MAGGID MISHNEH, OFTEN CITED BY THE
NOVOMINSKER REBBE

TRUTH
FALSITY

UPRIGHTNESS

"Vayivchar be'emes mipnei shehu emes — One should choose truth, simply because it is the truth." These words of the *Maggid Mishneh*, a 14th-century commentary on the Rambam's *Mishneh Torah*, were the mantra of the Novominsker Rebbe, **RABBI YAAKOV PERLOW** (1930-2020). The Rebbe would stress that *emes* is not only a means through which to create a *kiddush Hashem* by being impeccably honest in one's dealings and exemplary in one's behavior. Being truthful has intrinsic value as well. We must maintain our high standards of being *anshei emes,* people of truth, for the simple reason that it is the right thing to do.

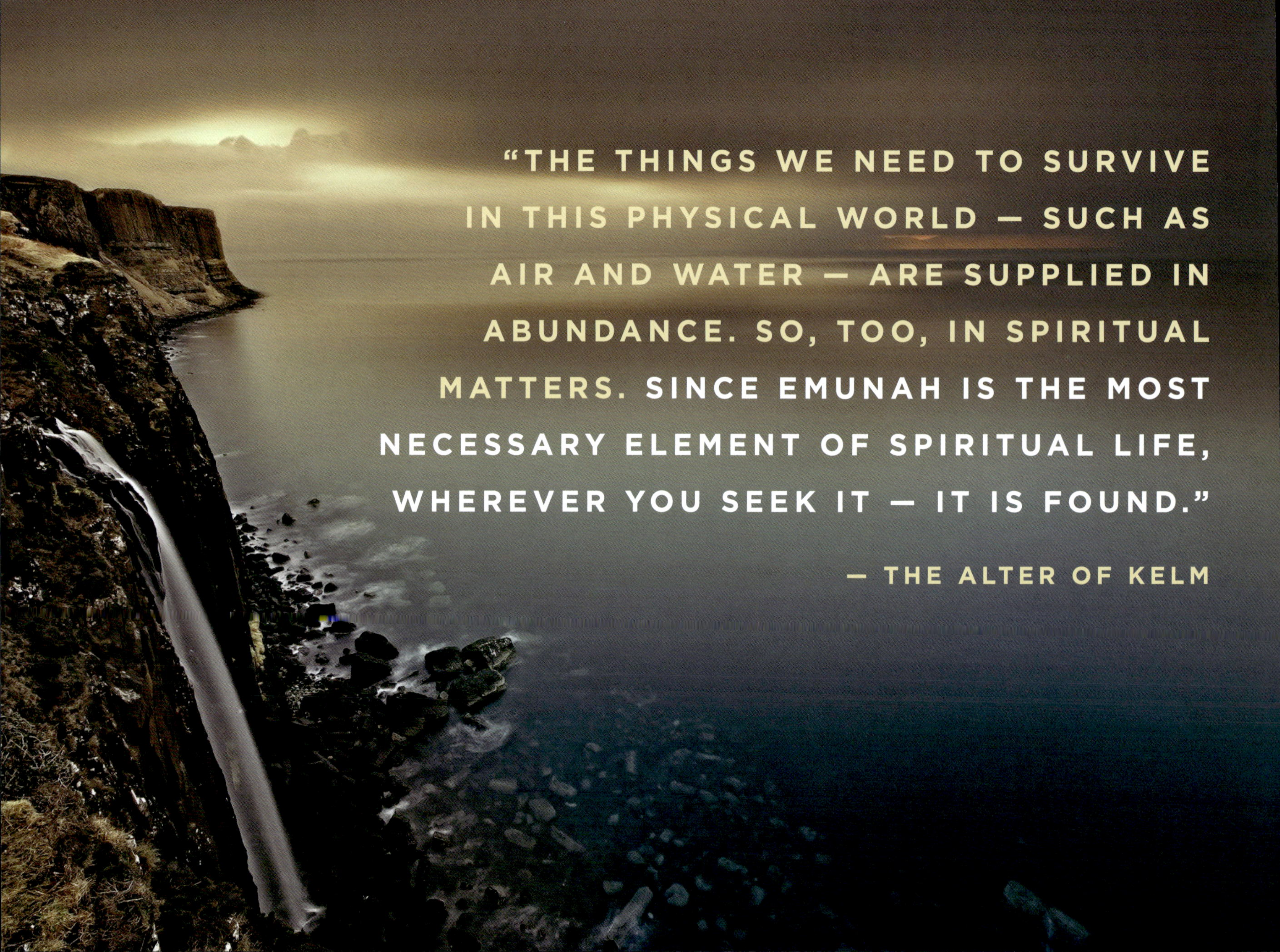

"THE THINGS WE NEED TO SURVIVE IN THIS PHYSICAL WORLD — SUCH AS AIR AND WATER — ARE SUPPLIED IN ABUNDANCE. SO, TOO, IN SPIRITUAL MATTERS. SINCE EMUNAH IS THE MOST NECESSARY ELEMENT OF SPIRITUAL LIFE, WHEREVER YOU SEEK IT — IT IS FOUND."
— THE ALTER OF KELM

UNIVERSAL

The *Chovos HaLevavos* (*Shaar HaBechinah* ch. 5) observes that God made air abundant and free of charge because of its indispensability to human survival. The Alter of Kelm, **RABBI SIMCHA ZISSEL ZIV BROIDE** (1824-1898) extends this principle to emunah. Since faith is so essential — without it we could not get through life — it is provided without limit. Those who wish to believe will find clear signs of Hashem's Presence in everything they do.

"LIKE A CHILD CLUTCHING HIS PARENT'S HAND, HASHEM LEADS US TO EXACTLY THE RIGHT DESTINATION."
— RABBI YERUCHAM LEVOVITZ

GUIDANCE

Eliezer, servant of Avraham, was sent by his master to find a shidduch for Yitzchak. After meeting Rivkah, the perfect mate for Yitzchak, Eliezer declares, "Hashem has led me along the journey" (*Bereishis* 24:27). The understanding is that Eliezer felt as if Hashem was leading him by the hand along his entire journey, without ever being lost or confused, from beginning to end. The Mashgiach of the Mir Yeshivah in Poland, **RABBI YERUCHAM LEVOVITZ** (1873-1936), explains that such Divine guidance is evident to any person who pays attention, and he provided his students with several personal examples of when he was steered along on his journey clearly with Divine guidance.

Siberian gulag

DETERMINATION

The brilliant Torah scholar **RABBI YECHEZKEL ABRAMSKY** (1886-1976) was imprisoned in a frigid Siberian gulag on trumped-up charges. Cast into a dark world, without family, students, *sefarim*, and the normal amenities he was used to, his spirits were low. When he awoke one morning, he recited the *Modeh Ani* prayer, thanking God for returning his soul to him. Just then, Rabbi Abramsky thought, "*Modeh ani*? Am I truly thankful for my soul being returned to me this morning in this dreadful place?" However, when he reached the end of the prayer, *rabbah emunasecha* (abundant is Your faithfulness), he was comforted. He interpreted these words homiletically, that even in the horrible reality in which he found himself, he still had the abundant, precious mitzvah of... *emunah!*

"THE PRIMARY PURPOSE
FOR THE GIVING OF
THE TORAH IS SO THAT
WE PLACE OUR TRUST
IN HASHEM, FOR THE
BASIS OF EVERYTHING IS
BITACHON…"

— THE VILNA GAON

FOUNDATIONAL

When the unparalleled master of Torah **RABBI ELIYAHU OF VILNA** (1720-1797), the Vilna Gaon, instructs us that the main purpose of Torah is bitachon, we get an idea of just how important it is to place our full trust and reliance in Hashem. Rabbi Chaim Friedlander, (*Sifsei Chaim*) explains this statement to mean that the purpose of all our service to Hashem is to perfect our bitachon in Him. The Torah was given to us in the merit of our bitachon, having accepted it without asking any questions — *na'aseh v'nishma*. However, only through studying and obeying the Torah can we perfect our bitachon and pass it on to future generations.

"A JEW DOESN'T GET BROKEN;
HE BECOMES BETTER."
— RABBI MOSHE FEINSTEIN
Photo credit:
Moshe D. Yarmish

RESILIENCE

A yeshivah *bachur* whose close friend
died suddenly was shaken to the core. He
approached the *Gadol HaDor*, **RABBI MOSHE
FEINSTEIN** (1895-1986), for consolation. "Rosh
Yeshivah, *ich bin tzubrochen;* I am so broken.
I need *chizuk*, strength." Lovingly, Rav Moshe
responded, "*Ah Yid vert nit tzubrochen. A Yid
vert besser.*" A Jew is resilient; he reacts to
tragedy by finding ways to improve, not by
becoming shattered and broken...

"'WHEN YOU GO OUT TO WAR... AND SEE HORSES AND CHARIOTS — FORCES SUPERIOR TO YOURS — HAVE NO FEAR OF THEM...' (DEVARIM 20:1). WHEN BRACING ONESELF FOR ANY IMMINENT THREAT, THE HEART SHOULD SENSE HASHEM'S SALVATION, AND

COMPOSURE

RABBEINU YONAH (1200-1263), in his Mussar classic *Shaarei Teshuvah*, explains that this verse, regarding the confidence in God one must have when going out to war, extends beyond the battlefield, to any arena of life in which there is overwhelming stress. The "horses and chariots" can come in the form of illness, financial pressure, or any other woe. The Torah teaches us not to be frightened; Hashem is with you. Trust in Him, follow Him, and everything will turn out well in the end.

"NO ONE IN THE WORLD IS WEALTHIER THAN ONE WHO STUDIES SHAAR HABITACHON; NO ONE IS HAPPIER THAN SOMEONE WHO HAS FAITH."

— RABBI YITZCHAK ZEV SOLOVEITCHIK

When the Brisker Rav, **RABBI YITZCHAK ZEV SOLOVEITCHIK** (1886-1959), got married, his affluent father-in-law presented him with an entire street in Warsaw, as a dowry. The many obligations of being a property owner made the Brisker Rav realize that his assets were taking him away from Torah study, and so he hired an agent to sell them. Just then, the First World War broke out and the Rav had to flee. When he returned to Warsaw, the agent was no longer among the living. The Rav went to the government archives to see what happened to his property, and was stunned to discover that the corrupt agent had put the street, with all its houses, in his own name. To strengthen himself, the Brisker Rav began studying *Shaar HaBitachon* (Gate of Trust) from the *sefer Chovos HaLevavos* many times. He would say, "I used to think that someone who owns a street in Warsaw is wealthy. Now I know that someone who studies *Shaar HaBitachon* repeatedly is wealthy, because bitachon makes a person stay calm. No one in the world is happier than someone who has bitachon."

“WITH EMUNAH, THERE ARE NO QUESTIONS.

ILLUMINATE

The saintly Chofetz Chaim, **RABBI YISRAEL MEIR KAGAN** (1838-1933), was a wellspring of emunah, instilling pure and absolute faith in the heart of his nation. He would often say, "With emunah, there are no questions; without emunah, there are no answers." When a person lives with emunah, life's many complexities and doubts do not plague him, for he knows that God is in full control of everything that transpires. Without emunah in one's life, however, the many mysteries of life go unsolved, for the truth eludes them... emunah lights up the darkness of life.

"STUDYING TORAH BOLSTERS EMUNAH; SO EVIDENT IS IT THAT THE TORAH IS FROM HASHEM."

— RABBI ELIYAHU DESSLER

BEDROCK

One assured way to develop genuine emunah is to engage in rigorous Torah learning. When engrossed in its study, our intrinsic faith is rekindled, says **RABBI ELIYAHU DESSLER** (1892-1953), a leading Mussar personality. The Torah's holy aura and penetrating brilliance leads one to the unmistakable conclusion that this is the word of God. Indeed, it is reported that towering *Gedolim* such as the Chofetz Chaim (1838-1933), Rabbi Elchonon Wasserman (1875-1941), and Rabbi Elazar Menachem Mann Shach (1899-2001) would reinforce their emunah by studying Chumash, particularly the beginning of the Torah — the story of Creation. Reading these Divine words as would a young child instilled in them an *emunah peshutah*, a faith pure and firm.

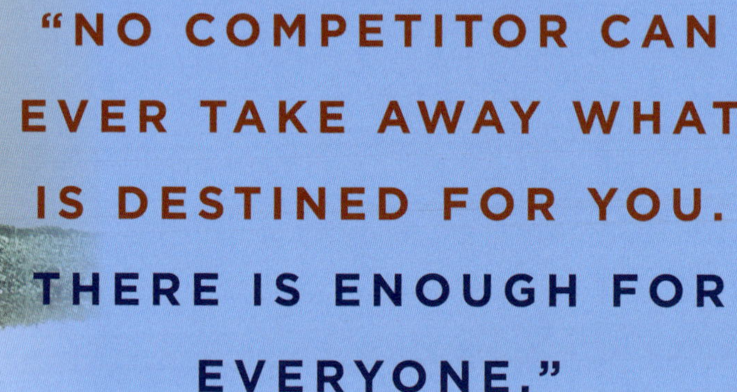
"NO COMPETITOR CAN EVER TAKE AWAY WHAT IS DESTINED FOR YOU. THERE IS ENOUGH FOR EVERYONE."

— RABBI MEIR OF PREMISHLAN

PLENTY

A desperate storeowner once approached
RABBI MEIR OF PREMISHLAN (1783-1850),
the Chassidic giant, complaining that
someone opened a similar store right next to
his, and he feared that his business would be
taken away. R' Meir softly replied, "Have you
ever seen a horse drink water from a river? He
walks into the water and stamps his hooves.
He does this because as he looks down at the
water, he sees his own reflection, and thinks
that another horse is also drinking. Afraid that
the "other" horse will consume all the water,
he kicks his mirror image. That is what a horse
does; you, however, know better — that there
is enough water in the river for all the horses,
and that no one can touch what Hashem has
prepared for him and for his friend. Place your
trust in Hashem and you will have nothing to
fear..."

"HASHEM DOES NOT CHALLENGE MAN WITH SOMETHING HE CANNOT HANDLE."
— RABBI EZRA ATTIYA

The Gemara in *Kesubos* (33b) compares death with torture, saying that the former is easier than the latter: "Even though Chananya, Mishael and Azaryah were ready to give up their lives but not bow down to an idol, had the enemy whipped them, they would have bowed." One of the towering Sephardic leaders of recent times, **RABBI EZRA ATTIYA** (1885-1970), asks why this criticism of those three great *tzaddikim* was necessary. He explains that the Gemara wants to teach us a vital lesson. A person will not be tested in life unless Hashem knows he can withstand it. Since Chananya, Mishael and Azaryah could not have handled the challenge of being flogged, they were not given that test!

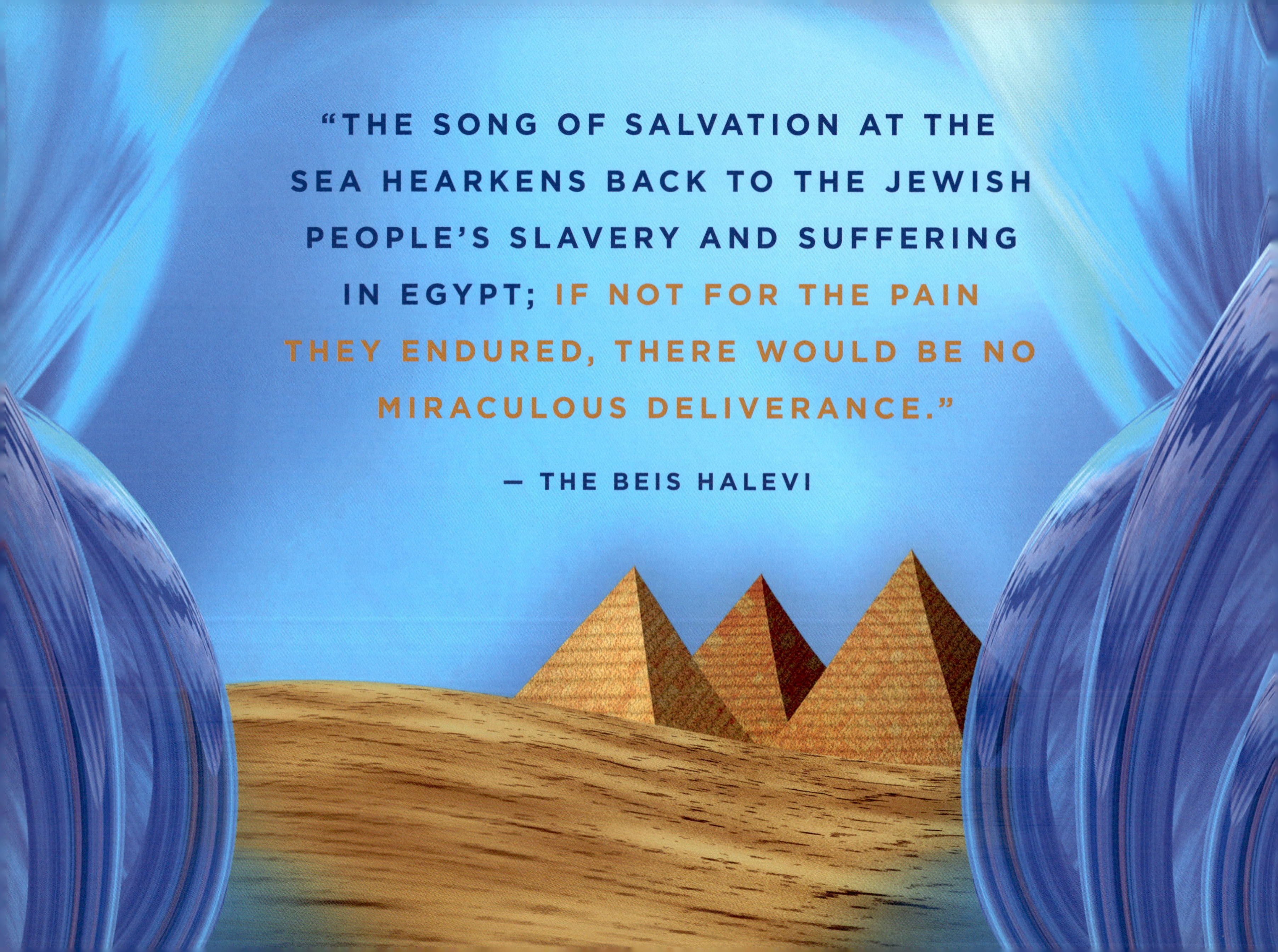

"THE SONG OF SALVATION AT THE SEA HEARKENS BACK TO THE JEWISH PEOPLE'S SLAVERY AND SUFFERING IN EGYPT; IF NOT FOR THE PAIN THEY ENDURED, THERE WOULD BE NO MIRACULOUS DELIVERANCE."
— THE BEIS HALEVI

INSTRUMENTAL

When the sea miraculously split before the Jewish people, they sang a glorious song of praise to Hashem for their freedom from Egypt, where they were slaves. Their very first word of song, *"Az,"* alluded, according to the Midrash, to their darkest hour of bondage. **RABBI YOSEF DOV SOLOVEITCHIK** (1820-1892), the Beis HaLevi, explains that a Jew must demonstrate gratitude not just for the salvation at hand, but for the suffering that preceded it, as well. We are thankful for the fact that we maintained our faith in God even at our national nadir, and that through our miraculous redemption from the shackles of Egypt we have become instruments to sanctify God's Name in the eyes of all.

"AS LONG AS THE CANDLE STILL BURNS, IT IS STILL POSSIBLE TO MAKE REPAIRS."

— RABBI YISRAEL OF SALANT

DILIGENCE

Late one night, the founder of the Mussar movement, **RABBI YISRAEL LIPKIN OF SALANT** (1810-1883), walked past the store of an old shoemaker, who was hunched over his workbench, doing his job by the light of a dwindling candle. When the Rav asked him why he is still at work at this late hour, the cobbler replied, "As long as the candle is still burning, it is still possible to work and to make repairs." His words struck Rav Yisrael like a thunderbolt, as he took them as a profound Mussar lesson for life. As long as the "candle" — our soul — is still burning, as long as Hashem has granted us the priceless gift of life, it is still possible to work and to make repairs, to perform our Divine mission and improve ourselves.

"WE MUST BE LIKE AN AIRPLANE, SLOWLY GAINING MOMENTUM UNTIL WE LIFT OFF HEAVENWARD."

— RABBI YEHUDAH ZEV SEGAL

ASCENT

The *tzaddik* **RABBI YEHUDAH ZEV SEGAL** (1910-1993), the Manchester Rosh Yeshivah, discovered Mussar lessons even in the everyday aspects of life. Once on an airplane, he made the following observation. "A plane warms up its engines, gains momentum on the ground, and finally lifts up into the sky. We have to be the same way, intensifying our service little by little until we are ready to raise ourselves Heavenward in *d'veikus* (Divine attachment) with our Creator!"

"WHATEVER MUST HAPPEN
— HAPPENS.
AND WHATEVER HAPPENS...
IS FOR THE GOOD."

— RABBI AHARON KOTLER

ACCEPTANCE

A few days before the passing of the Rosh Yeshivah of Lakewood, **RABBI AHARON KOTLER** (1891-1962), after months of suffering from the dreaded disease, his Rebbetzin tried to comfort and encourage him. *"Es vet zein gutt,"* she said, "it will turn out good." The Rosh Yeshivah immediately responded, *"Ess iz* shoin *gut* — it is *already* good!" He then added a fundamental principle of faith: *"Vos darf zein… iz, vos iz… iz gutt.* Whatever must take place, is taking place (i.e., the way Hashem wants it to be); and whatever is taking place is, therefore, good." Rav Aharon had absolute faith that everything Hashem does is for the good and there is no reason to fear. Shortly before his passing, he declared, "I'm in good hands."

The Brisker Rav (right) walking with
two of his sons

"WHEN A PERSON FOCUSES ON THE VERSE, 'HASHEM, HE IS GOD, THERE IS NOTHING ELSE BESIDES HIM' (DEVARIM 4:35), HE WILL BE PROTECTED FROM ALL HARMFUL FORCES."

— RABBI CHAIM OF VOLOZHIN

ARMOR

In his *sefer Nefesh HaChaim*, the founder of the Volozhin Yeshivah, **RABBI CHAIM OF VOLOZHIN** (1749-1821), writes that if a person finds himself in danger and internalizes that there is nothing else besides Hashem, he will be protected. Although such forces pose a threat, with absolute faith in Hashem they are relegated to nothing but puppets in the hands of God. The Brisker Rav, Rabbi Yitzchak Zev Soloveitchik (1886-1959), attested to the fact that following this teaching of the Nefesh HaChaim spared him from harm on more than one occasion. When he was ordered, as a young man, to appear before the Russian draft board to be inducted into the Czar's army, he focused on "*Ein od milvado*," and was exempted. Also, during WWII, he traveled the roads of Europe unharmed by the Nazis who stood at every bend, through focusing on the sovereignty of Hashem.

"DOES ADDING AN EXTRA SPIGOT TO A BARREL INCREASE THE AMOUNT OF WINE INSIDE?"

— THE CHOFETZ CHAIM

EXERTION

A person must decide how much time to devote to earning a livelihood. True, *hishtadlus*, human effort, is necessary, but beyond a certain point, it is considered an excessive use of his time, which should be better put toward spiritual endeavors. After all, Hashem is the true Provider, and one's income has been Divinely predetermined on Rosh Hashanah. The Chofetz Chaim, **RABBI YISRAEL MEIR KAGAN** (1838-1933), used a parable of a barrel of wine with a single spigot. The foolish owner drills another hole into the barrel and attaches a second spigot, in the hopes that he will thereby double his output. While the wine came out twice as fast, his barrel emptied in half the time, gaining him nothing from his extraneous effort.

Courtesy of Chofetz Chaim Heritage Foundation

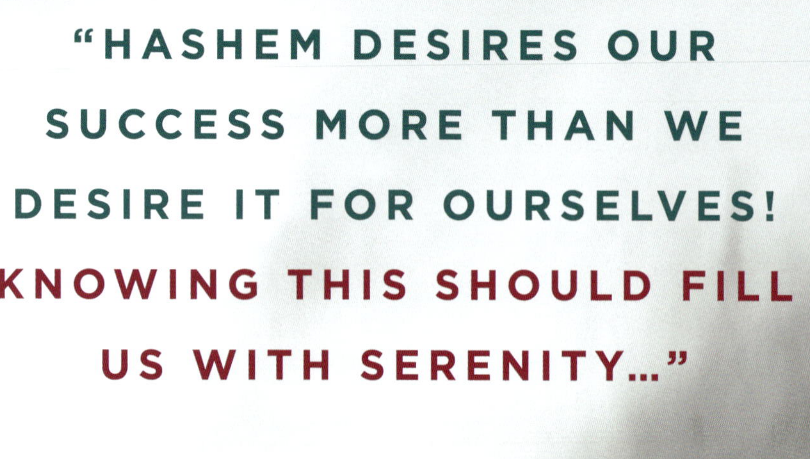

"HASHEM DESIRES OUR SUCCESS MORE THAN WE DESIRE IT FOR OURSELVES! KNOWING THIS SHOULD FILL US WITH SERENITY..."

— RABBI MEIR SIMCHA HAKOHEN OF DVINSK

TRIUMPH

In his masterwork *Meshech Chochmah*, **RABBI MEIR SIMCHA HAKOHEN OF DVINSK** (1843-1926) speaks of the degree to which a person should be relaxed and at peace in life. Does the king's son worry about his livelihood? Of course not! He knows that his father will always provide for his needs. Likewise, God is our King and our Father, and will therefore be our salvation. R' Meir Simcha continues that the Almighty is concerned for us in times of trouble, and desires our success in times of good, even *more* than we do for ourselves! Should we not feel peaceful and secure at all times?

"CHINUCH IS PRIMARILY TO INSTILL EMUNAH IN OUR CHILDREN, AND TO RAISE THEM KNOWING THAT WHATEVER WE GIVE THEM IS A GIFT FROM HIM..."
— RABBI MOSHE FEINSTEIN

In a letter, the leading Torah luminary **RABBI MOSHE FEINSTEIN** (1895-1986) stressed the importance of implanting emunah in one's children. He writes, "The primary aspect of *chinuch* is to raise one's children with emunah in Hashem and His Torah, and in the belief that whatever one possesses is a gift from Hashem. Then the child will acquire a love of Hashem and of his parents, who are Heaven's emissaries to grant him his needs. In this way, he will carry out what he is told with love, with an understanding that he is fulfilling the will of Hashem…"

"ONE MUST NEVER TAKE REVENGE; THE WRONG DONE TO YOU WAS ORDAINED BY GOD."

— SEFER HACHINUCH

RECONCILE

The Torah prohibits taking revenge and
bearing a grudge against a fellow Jew. The
simple reason for this is that it will ratchet
up tension and strife among our people. The
13th century *Sefer HaChinuch,* though, adds
a deeper meaning behind this prohibition.
Everything that happens to a person — either
good or bad — comes upon him from God.
Therefore, when someone causes another
person pain or suffering, it was actually God
Who decreed that those woes come upon
him, to atone for his sins. It therefore makes
no sense to take revenge upon the person
who wronged you, for that person was, in fact,
not the cause of your suffering.

"INSTEAD OF ASKING GOD 'LAMAH — WHY?' WE ASK 'L'MAH — TOWARD WHAT END IS THIS?' HOW CAN I LEARN AND GROW FROM IT?"
— RABBI SAMSON RAPHAEL HIRSCH

LESSON

RABBI SAMSON RAPHAEL HIRSCH (1808-1888), the noted German Torah leader and thinker, notes in his commentary to *Tehillim* (22:2) that King David, when asking "*Keli Keli lamah azavtani* — My God, my God, why have you forsaken me," actually uses the grammar indicating that his question is not *why* but *toward what end*. The anguish and suffering I have endured, the tests and the challenges I have faced, what am I to do with them? Indeed, a Jew does not ask questions of 'why.' He trusts that God has His reasons, and it is not our place to question Him. What one *may* ask is *L'Mah* — what can I take from this experience to grow, accomplish something positive, and get closer to Hashem?

"DURING THE MONTH OF ELUL, THE KING IS IN THE FIELD."
— THE BAAL HATANYA

PROXIMITY

Elul is the extraordinary month of introspection and preparation prior to the Days of Judgment from Rosh Hashanah until Yom Kippur. To explain the unique nature of Elul, the Baal HaTanya, **RABBI SHNEUR ZALMAN OF LIADI** (1745-1812), uses a parable of a king being in a field. Permission is granted to anyone who desires to approach him and meet. This opportunity for closeness is a golden one, but it does not last forever. Once the king returns to his royal palace, one will need a formal invitation to have an audience with him. This is what Elul is. Hashem makes Himself available to every Jew during this holy month — *HaMelech Basadeh*. Unparalleled closeness to the King is possible while He is still "in the field," before He returns to His Heavenly palace to sit on His Throne of Judgment...

Credit: Rami Sharabi

"THE MORE I DISCUSS EMUNAH — THE MORE I BELIEVE!"
— RABBI MORDECHAI OF LECHOWITZ

COMMUNICATE

"*He'emanti ki adaber* — I have kept faith, although I say..." (*Tehillim* 116:10). The Chassidic master **RABBI MORDECHAI OF LECHOWITZ** (1742-1810) interprets this verse homiletically, that "My faith is strengthened *because* I speak [of matters of faith]." Conversing about emunah, recounting stories of *Hashgachah Pratis* (Divine Providence), reminding ourselves and those around us about Who runs the world, are important ways to fortify one's faith in Hashem.

"ANY HEARTFELT PRAYER MUST BE ANSWERED. IT CAN'T BE OTHERWISE."

— THE STEIPLER GAON

ASSURED

When Rabbi Shneur Kotler (1918-1982), Rosh Yeshivah of Beis Medrash Govoha of Lakewood, suffered from a terminal illness, a group of his students traveled to Bnei Brak, to ask the holy Steipler Gaon, **RABBI YAAKOV YISRAEL KANIEVSKY** (1899-1985), to intensify his prayers on his behalf. They confided to the Steipler that they were discouraged that despite the tens of thousands of Jewish people praying so fervently, the Rosh Yeshivah's condition continued to deteriorate. The Steipler told them not to be dismayed, as all sincere prayers must be answered. If they are not answered today, they will be answered tomorrow. If not tomorrow, in a week, a month, a year, one hundred years or more... One cannot say for sure when a prayer will be answered, said the Steipler, but we can be assured that every prayer will be answered somehow, someday.

"I KNOW THE SUN WILL RISE TOMORROW MORNING. NOT BECAUSE IT ROSE YESTERDAY, BUT BECAUSE HASHEM ASSURED US IN THE TORAH (BEREISHIS 8:22), 'DAY AND NIGHT SHALL NOT CEASE.'"
— THE CHOFETZ CHAIM

GUARANTEE

Most people base their assumptions and predictions on studies, statistics, and science. To the Chofetz Chaim, **RABBI YISRAEL MEIR KAGAN** (1838-1933), however, nothing was assured unless the Torah stated it. How did he know that the sun would rise tomorrow? Not because it rose yesterday, but because Hashem told Noach following the Deluge that day and night would no longer cease. The Torah's words are what determine the reality. The Chofetz Chaim would extend this notion to the arrival of Mashiach. "The same way I am sure the sun will rise tomorrow due to a verse in the Torah, I fully believe Mashiach will come because the Torah guarantees it" (see *Bamidbar* 14:21).

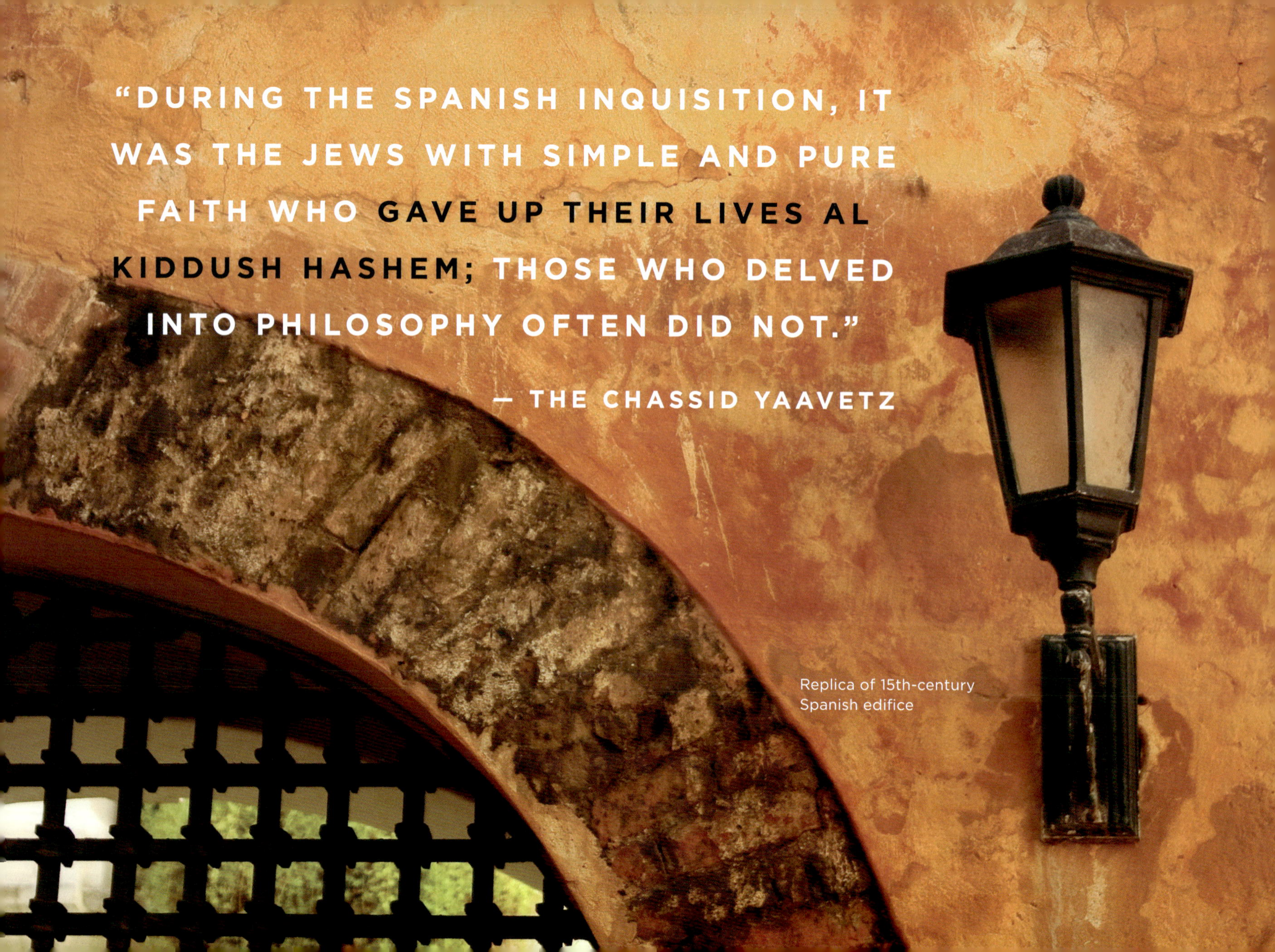

Replica of 15th-century Spanish edifice

UNWAVERING

 The Chassid Yaavetz, **RABBI YOSEF YAAVETZ** (15th-16th century), was born in Spain and left during the Expulsion in 1492. He witnessed, during the Spanish Inquisition, that in times of forced conversions, while Jewish philosophers were less likely to cling to their faith and die as martyrs, the common Jewish folk imbued with a pure, simple faith willingly yielded their lives *al Kiddush Hashem*. Serving Hashem based on the *mesorah* they received from their fathers and grandfathers, the "simple" Jews possessed a level of emunah and bitachon in Hashem that was resolute. Those who delved in philosophy, however, were less firm and steadfast in their belief, and would often bend when coerced by torture or death. The Bnei Yissaschar explains that this is because emunah based on finite human understanding will be finite as well, and when put to the test will often fail. However, emunah based on the absolute belief in the infinite God will likewise be infinite, and no amount of torture or intimidation will break it.

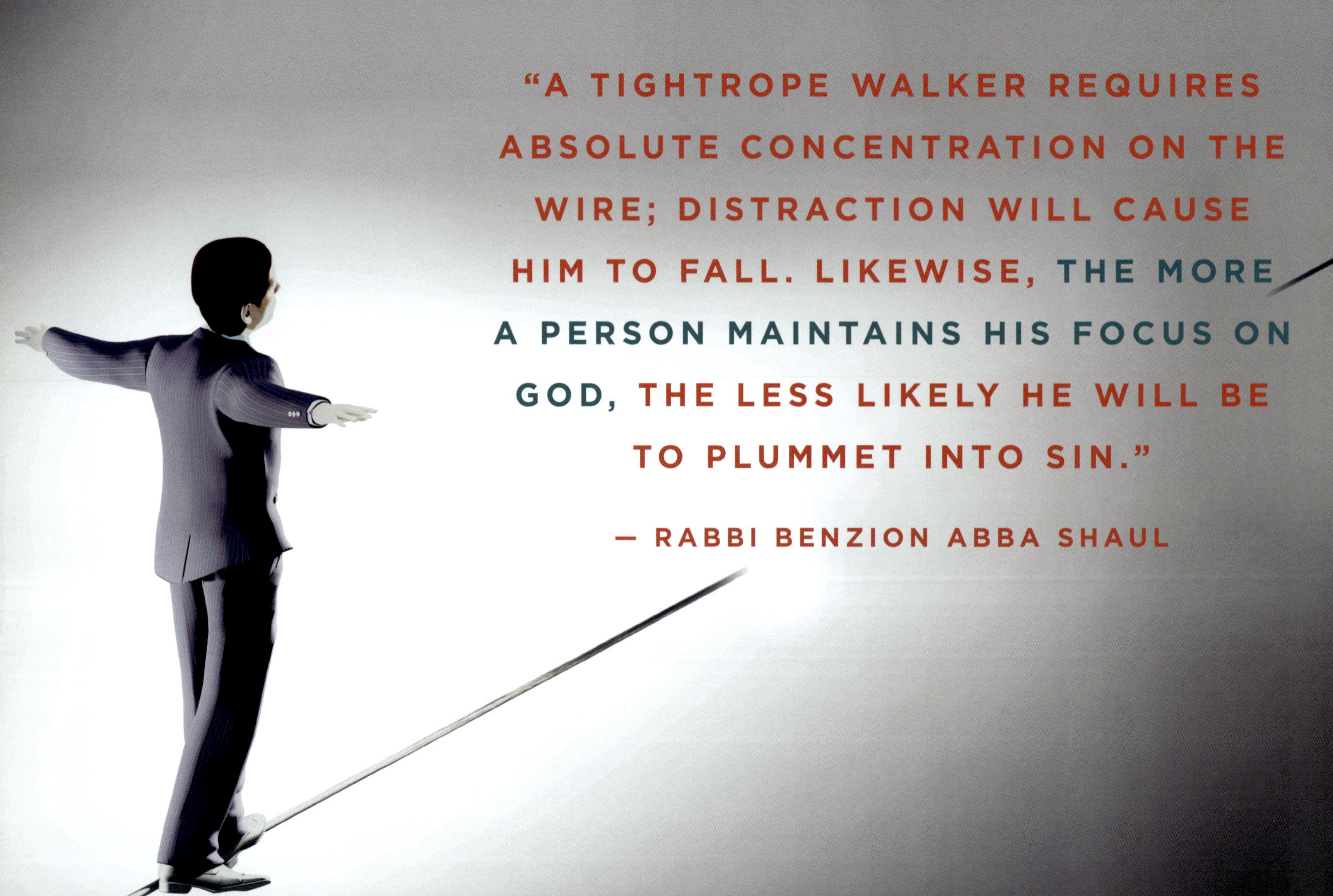

"A TIGHTROPE WALKER REQUIRES ABSOLUTE CONCENTRATION ON THE WIRE; DISTRACTION WILL CAUSE HIM TO FALL. LIKEWISE, THE MORE A PERSON MAINTAINS HIS FOCUS ON GOD, THE LESS LIKELY HE WILL BE TO PLUMMET INTO SIN."
— RABBI BENZION ABBA SHAUL

The highest level achievable for a servant of Hashem is maintaining constant awareness that he is in His Presence, as King David writes (*Tehillim* 16:8), "I have set Hashem before me always." Were one to stay focused on this reality at all times, he would not stumble into sin. The Rosh Yeshivah of Porat Yosef, **RABBI BENZION ABBA SHAUL** (1924-1998), compares this to the absolute concentration required to walk across a high wire; the moment the walker begins to think about something other than maintaining his balance on the rope before him, he is bound to fall...

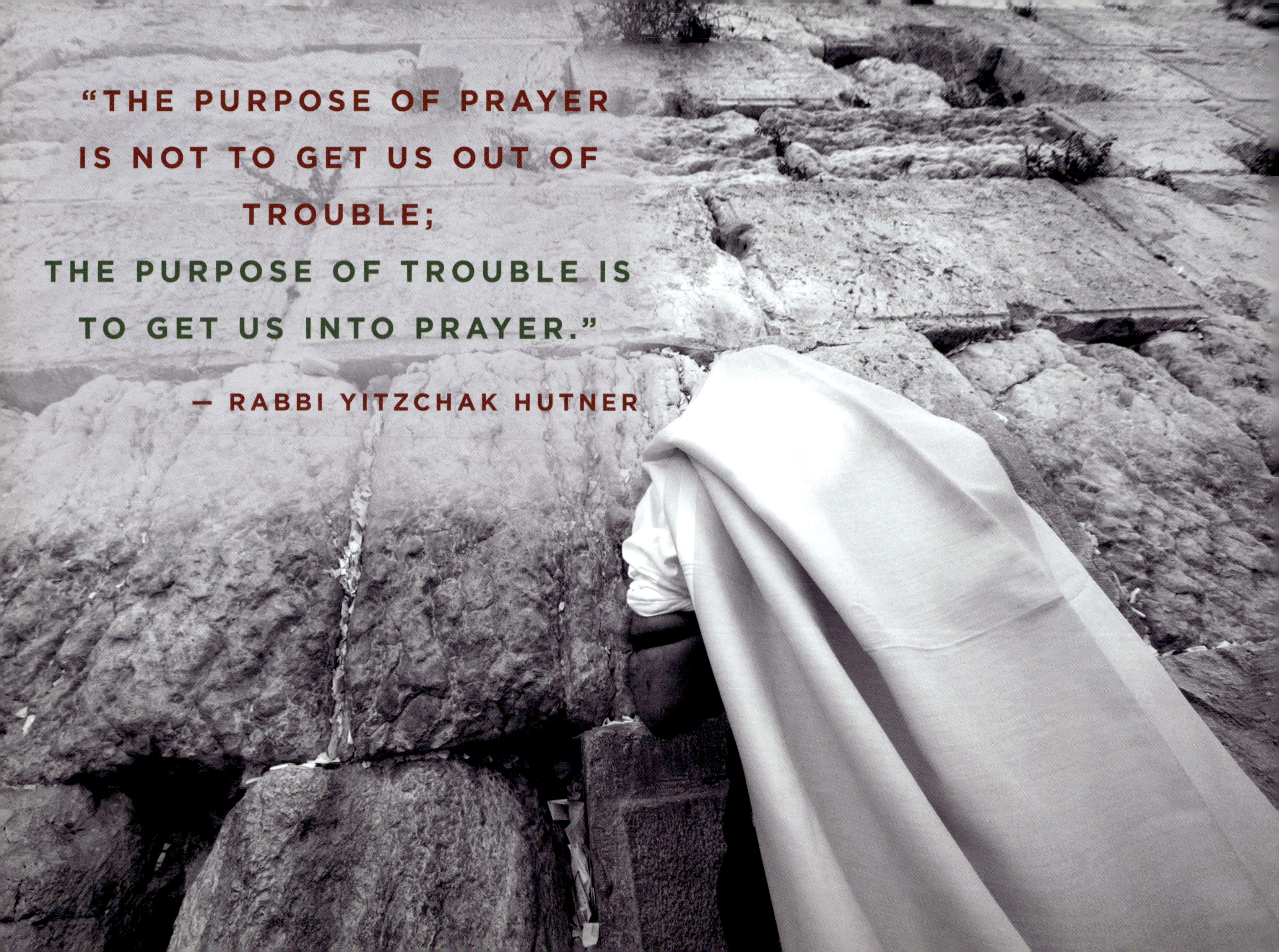

"THE PURPOSE OF PRAYER IS NOT TO GET US OUT OF TROUBLE; THE PURPOSE OF TROUBLE IS TO GET US INTO PRAYER."
— RABBI YITZCHAK HUTNER

It is commonly believed that fervent prayer is a reactive response to an emergency: somebody takes ill — open a Tehillim and pray! **RABBI YITZCHAK HUTNER** (1906-1980), Rosh Yeshivas Rabbeinu Chaim Berlin, infers from a Midrash that when it comes to *tzaddikim*, there are times that it starts the other way. Hashem desires, as it were, the heartfelt prayers of the righteous — *HaKadosh Baruch Hu mis'aveh l'tefillasam shel tzaddikim.* When Hashem wants to bring out their prayer and passion at a particular time, He casts a crisis upon them, rousing them to pour out their heart in supplication. Once His wish has been satisfied, the calamity should subside.

"I NEVER THOUGHT ABOUT WHETHER I COULD DO SOMETHING, BUT ONLY ABOUT WHETHER I HAD TO DO IT. IF SOMETHING HAD TO BE DONE, I KNEW THAT GOD WILL GIVE THE MEANS OF DOING IT."
— RABBI YOSEF YOIZEL HURWITZ

AMBITION

The Alter of Novardok, **RABBI YOSEF YOIZEL HURWITZ** (1847-1919), was a man of remarkable achievements. After spending years in solitude, engaging in Torah study and deep introspection, he emerged from his ascetic, isolated life to establish more than eighty yeshivos (!), changing the Torah world of Eastern Europe. When asked about his remarkable ability to build Torah on such a scale unhampered by the doubts and fears weighing down others with similar ambitions, the Alter revealed that his prolific accomplishments were rooted in deep faith. Rather than thinking about his own capabilities, he thought about the spiritual *need* for the endeavor. Once he determined that it was imperative, he initiated the project, with full confidence that Hashem — Who directs everything — will facilitate its completion and success.

"EVERYTHING A PERSON SEES IN LIFE IS A MESSAGE TO HIM FROM ABOVE."

— THE BAAL SHEM TOV

RETURN NOW
תשובה עכשיו

NOTICE

In a world orchestrated by God, there are no such things as coincidences. While we no longer have prophets conveying to us the word of God, the **BAAL SHEM TOV** (1698-1760), founder of Chassidus, teaches us that Hashem still communicates with us. Through our daily experiences, interactions, and signs, Hashem teaches us vital lessons. We should observe all the events we go through each day and see them as significant, knowing that we are constantly being sent messages by the One above, Who cares for us and guides us with love.

שנת תרפ"   וווארשא, יום

קלונמים קלמיש שפירא

בהה"צ מוהר"א זצלל"ה

פיאסעצנע

"WHAT AM I LACKING? SIMPLY PUT,
TO BE A JEW. I HAVE ALL THE RIGHT
EXTERNALS, BUT LACK A SOUL…"

— RABBI KLONIMUS KALMAN SHAPIRA

AUTHENTICITY

RABBI KLONIMUS KALMAN SHAPIRA (1889-1943), the Piaseczna Rebbe, was a brilliant and inspiring Chassidic master, who served as a spiritual leader in the Warsaw Ghetto after the Nazi invasion of Poland in 1939 until he was martyred. On the 19th of Iyar 5689 (1929), as the Rebbe reached his 40th birthday, he penned a profound letter *to himself*, in which he undertook, on this milestone, to work on attaining the one elusive thing he felt he lacked — an authentic Jewish soul bound intimately with God. He concludes his letter with a prayer: "Master of the Universe, I confess to You Who observes all hidden matters, and before You I plead. I am cast so far from You — Your chambers are so distant from me. I simply wish to convert and from this day forward to become a Jew… help me so that I do not squander my remaining years… Draw me near to You, and allow me to enter Your inner chambers…"

"IF 25,000 JEWS AWAITING THE BEIS HALEVI WERE ENOUGH TO BRING HIM TO BRISK, WOULD THAT SAME NUMBER NOT SUFFICE TO BRING MASHIACH?"
— THE CHOFETZ CHAIM

YEARNING

One of the tenets of our faith is that we eagerly await Mashiach's arrival each day. But do we really do so, or are we all-too-comfortable in this exile? It is told that when the Beis HaLevi, Rabbi Yosef Dov Soloveitchik (1820-1892), was first offered the rabbinate of Brisk, he turned it down. Only once he was told that 25,000 Jews were eagerly awaiting his arrival at the train station in Brisk did he reconsider and accept the position. He said, "How can I disappoint 25,000 Jews?" The saintly Chofetz Chaim, **RABBI YISRAEL MEIR KAGAN** (1838-1933), would repeat this story to teach a critical lesson: If the Beis HaLevi could not refuse 25,000 Jews eagerly anticipating his arrival, certainly Mashiach can't either! We must conclude that even that number of Jews globally are not truly yearning for his arrival. If we would but await his arrival, arrive he would!

"EVEN IF MAN LIVED THOUSANDS OF YEARS, HE COULD NOT COMPREHEND THE EXTENT OF YOUR POWERFUL DEEDS."

— RABBI YISRAEL OF NAJARA

Rav Shach reciting *kinnos* on Tishah B'Av

UNFATHOMABLE

Rabbi Elazar Menachem Mann Shach (1899-2001), revered Rosh Yeshivah of Ponevezh, once tried to relieve someone's sorrow and fortify him with words of hope and trust in God. He then requested that a siddur be brought to him. He turned the pages to the *zemer* of *Kah Ribon,* composed by **RABBI YISRAEL OF NAJARA** (1555-1625) and, with great feeling, began reading *lu yichyeh... Even if man lived thousands of years, he could not comprehend the extent of Your powerful deeds.* Repeatedly he recited the words, *"He could not comprehend the extent of Your powerful deeds."* Tears streamed down the Rosh Yeshivah's face as his frail body wept uncontrollably.

"FAITH IS NOT ABOUT EVERYTHING TURNING OUT ALRIGHT; IT IS ABOUT BEING ALRIGHT NO MATTER HOW THINGS TURN OUT."

— THE CHAZON ISH

PERSEVERE

Many people understand bitachon to mean that when faced with an undecided future with an outcome either good or bad, one trusts in Hashem that surely the good result will occur. While eminent authorities espouse this definition of bitachon, the Chazon Ish, **RABBI AVRAHAM YESHAYA KARELITZ** (1878-1953), felt otherwise. We do not have prophets to tell us what will happen, and man is not privy to the final decisions of Hashem. Rather, says the Chazon Ish, bitachon is knowing that nothing happens by chance, and that whatever does transpire, we believe to be the decree of Hashem; we will accept it as His will.

"EMUNAH IS LIKE A TREE;
BITACHON IS LIKE THE
FRUIT OF THAT TREE."

— THE RAMBAN

In describing the difference between the closely-related concepts of emunah (faith) and bitachon (reliance), the Ramban, **RABBEINU MOSHE BEN NACHMAN** (1194-1270), explains that bitachon is an outgrowth of emunah. Firmly *believing* in Hashem's existence enables a person to completely *rely* on Hashem to fulfill his needs. Just as a tree may not yield fruit, but all fruit comes from a tree, so he who possesses emunah does not necessarily possess bitachon, yet one with bitachon must have emunah. In the words of the Ramban, "Everyone who trusts surely believes, but not everyone who believes, trusts."

"DO NOT SAY SOMEONE WAS LATE AND MISSED HIS TRAIN — HE SIMPLY CAME EARLY FOR THE NEXT TRAIN! EVERYTHING IS IN THE HANDS OF HEAVEN."
— RABBI YOSEF YOIZEL HURWITZ

PRECISION

Hashgachah Pratis, Divine Providence, is a balm that soothes the troubled spirit. By viewing — and internalizing — every occurrence of life as being ordained by God, a person would not be anguished or unsettled. The Alter of Novardok, **RABBI YOSEF YOIZEL HURWITZ** (1847-1919), provided a common example of how refocusing our perspective can make us calmer, happier people. When a person rushes to catch a train and misses it by seconds, he feels disappointment and frustration ("So close!"; "Now I'll be late for my meeting!") But that, insisted the Mussar giant, is the wrong way of looking at it. Hashem, in His infinite wisdom, knew that he was not destined to board the first train, for reasons only He knows. Instead, the person was supposed to catch the second train — for which he is early! Taking the second train — and not the first — will bring him to his destination at precisely the moment that the Conductor has scheduled for him.

"WE WHO SURVIVED THE WAR WERE, IN TRUTH, MEANT TO BE KILLED ALONG WITH THE HOLY SIX MILLION. IF WE WERE SPARED IT IS FOR ONE REASON — TO RESTORE THE JEWISH PEOPLE TO ITS FORMER GLORY..."
— RABBI YOSEF SHLOMO KAHANEMAN

The Ponevezher Rav, **RABBI YOSEF SHLOMO KAHANEMAN** (1886-1969), rebuilt his illustrious community of Ponevezh, Lithuania — annihilated by the Nazis — on the holy soil of Bnei Brak. He was once addressing a crowd of people following the war, and cried, "We are *nosarim* — remnants!" He explained that after the death of Aaron's two sons, Nadav and Avihu, the verse says (*Vayikra* 10:12), "Moshe spoke to Aharon and to Elazar and Isamar," Aharon's "left over children" (*banav hanosarim*). Rashi adds, "They were left over from death. This teaches that death was decreed upon them as well, but [they survived]." "We, who survived the war," asserted Rav Kahaneman, "were supposed to be killed as well, but we were 'left over,' and it is our sacred duty to do anything in our power to rebuild all that was destroyed…"

"EVERY JEW IS AN
'ONLY CHILD' IN THE
EYES OF GOD."

— THE BAAL SHEM TOV

When a person ponders his relationship with God, it is easy to mistakenly assume that he is merely a number. Since God is Father to countless others, perhaps a unique and special connection with each individual cannot be fostered. But, says the **BAAL SHEM TOV** (1698-1760), founder of Chassidus, one must realize that the nature of every Jew's relationship with Hashem is hardly that of a number — he is considered an only child! Hashem has endless love for each Jew; He takes pride in his every accomplishment.

"IF ONE GIVES GENEROUSLY TO THE NEEDY, HASHEM SEES THAT HE IS A GOOD TRUSTEE AND WILL ENTRUST HIM WITH EVEN GREATER RICHES!"

— RABBI SHIMON SHKOP

The Rosh Yeshivah of Grodno, **RABBI SHIMON SHKOP** (1860-1939), writes in his introduction to his classic *Shaarei Yosher* that when Hashem blesses a human being with wealth, He is actually appointing him as His treasurer to distribute funds to the needy. If he fulfills his duty properly, giving the appropriate tithes to the poor, Hashem raises his rank and appoints him over an even greater fortune to distribute, upward and upward, so that he can achieve his lofty desire to benefit the multitudes through his stewardship of the treasury.

"MAY THE CHOFETZ CHAIM SOON WALK BAREFOOT AND CARRY STONES..."
— RABBI YOSEF ZUNDEL HUTNER

RABBI YOSEF ZUNDEL HUTNER (1846-1899) of Eyshishok was a renowned *tzaddik*. It is told that when the Chofetz Chaim once sent a wagon driver to Rav Yosef Zundel to secure a blessing on his behalf, the Rav sent a cryptic wish that the Chofetz Chaim should soon "go barefoot and carry stones." To the simple wagon driver, the Rabbi of Eyshishok's words sounded more like a curse than a blessing, and he avoided the Chofetz Chaim, loath to share such a dire prediction with him. Finally, when the Chofetz Chaim summoned the driver and insisted on hearing the exact words of Rav Yosef Zundel, he was overjoyed. "I am a Kohen," the Chofetz Chaim explained. "The Eyshishok Rav blessed me that when the Beis HaMikdash is speedily rebuilt, I should merit to serve as the Kohen Gadol, walking barefoot while carrying on my heart the stones of the Choshen (Breastplate)…"

"BELIEVING IS GREATER THAN SEEING."

— THE CHIDDUSHEI HARIM

PERCEIVE

"Seeing is believing," goes the popular saying, meaning that one must see something before it can be accepted as reality. However, when it comes to emunah, says the Chiddushei HaRim of Ger, **RABBI YITZCHAK MEIR ROTENBERG-ALTER** (1799-1866), the opposite is true. Believing is actually *greater* than seeing! With the power of faith, one can see what the eyes do not! In fact, the Kotzker Rebbe commented about certain Rebbes who reportedly beheld the Ushpizin — the seven holy guests that visit our succah, "I don't see them, but I *believe* that they are in my succah, and belief is far clearer than seeing!"

"THE KEY TO BITACHON IS
PATIENCE..."
— RABBI YECHEZKEL LEVENSTEIN

ENDURANCE

The *Chovos HaLevavos*, in his introduction to *Shaar HaBitachon*, describes the essence of bitachon as feeling "serenity about worldly pressures and tranquility from the things that cause the mind to ache." Why, then, are we still nervous, if we believe in Hashem and trust that He is in charge? The Mashgiach of Mir and Ponevezh, **RABBI YECHEZKEL LEVENSTEIN** (1885-1974), suggests that our anxiety stems from a mistaken assumption that Hashem operates the world in the same manner as we do. When we wish to assist another, we do so spontaneously. The ways of Hashem are different; He gives a person a test and does not reveal His goodness until later. One needs to have patience when awaiting Hashem's salvation. It will come exactly when it is supposed to.

"TRUSTING IN HASHEM IS THE
GREATEST OCCUPATION…"

— CHOVOS HALEVAVOS

PROFESSION

The *Chovos HaLevavos* is the classic Mussar work, written by **RABBEINU BACHYA IBN PAKUDA** (c. 1050-1120). In his chapter entitled *Shaar HaBitachon* (Gate of Trust), he describes the immense benefits of trust in God in this world: a heart at rest, free of worldly cares; a tranquil spirit, undisturbed and untroubled by lack of bodily gratification; a sense of calm, security, and peace. He describes the many ways that one who depends on God makes a "living" even better than that of an alchemist — a person with the reputed ability to transform cheap metals into gold. [The modern-day equivalent of this would be a sophisticated currency counterfeiter, illegally printing money.] Though it seems like his livelihood is assured and limitless, he is always tense, fearful of being discovered, and distrustful of others. One who has absolute trust in God, on the other hand, has peace of mind that God will provide for him, enabling him to enjoy a good, wholesome, and fulfilling life.

"TAKE YOUR BLANKET IN LIFE AND
WARM OTHER PEOPLE WITH IT!"

— RABBI NOSSON TZVI FINKEL

In 2002, a group of successful not-yet-religious American Jewish businessmen had a private audience with **RABBI NOSSON TZVI FINKEL** (1943-2011), the late Mir Rosh Yeshivah, in Yerushalayim. When the Rosh Yeshivah entered the room, he asked them, "Who can tell me what the lesson of the Holocaust is?" When none of their answers satisfied R' Nosson Tzvi, he continued, "Okay gentlemen, let me tell you the essence of the human spirit. As the Jews in the concentration camps went into the barracks to sleep, only one person was given a blanket for every six cramped on the wooden boards called a bed. The person who received the blanket, when he went to bed, had to decide, 'Am I going to push the blanket to the other five people who did not get one, or am I going to pull it toward myself to stay warm?' It was during this defining moment that we learned the power of the human spirit, because we pushed the blanket to five others." And then the Rosh Yeshivah stood up and said to them, "Take your blanket. Take it back to America and push it to five other people."

"A SINGLE MITZVAH PERFORMED IN OUR DECADENT, IMMORAL TIMES IS EQUAL TO MANY 'BIG' MITZVOS DONE IN PREVIOUS GENERATIONS, WHEN THE RESISTANCE OF THE YETZER HARA WAS LESS FIERCE..."

— THE ARIZAL

ADVANTAGE

The holy Arizal, **RABBI YITZCHAK LURIA** (1534-1572), once explained to his main disciple, Rabbi Chaim Vital (1543-1620), that one's spiritual stature is not based solely on deeds; other considerations, such as the times and generation one lives in, are factored in as well. One cannot equate a mitzvah performed in an era of impurity and temptation, when the evil inclination is so formidable, with a mitzvah achieved when the world was more wholesome, less enticed by the yetzer hara's seduction. This explains how our generation can bring Mashiach even though he did not come in previous times graced by spiritual giants. Since our times are so morally challenging, it is entirely possible that our few good deeds can match, or even surpass, those of previous generations!

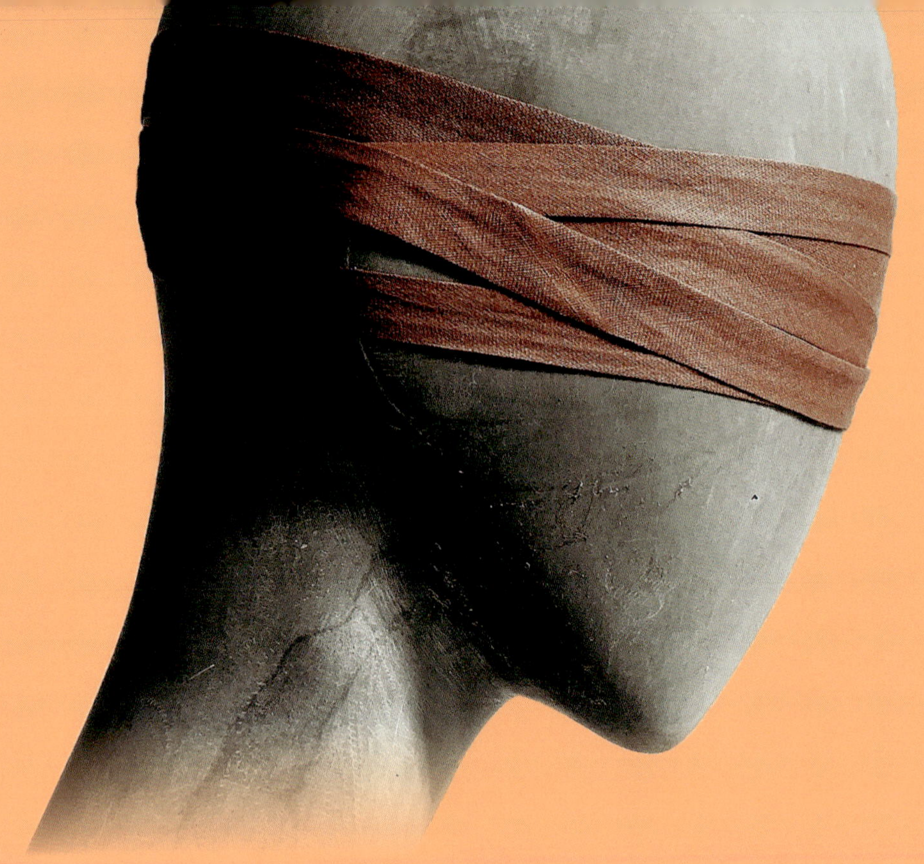

"THE EXISTENCE OF GOD IS CLEAR TO THE RATIONAL MIND, BUT PASSIONS OF THE HEART BLIND MAN FROM SEEING THAT TRUTH."

— RABBI ELCHONON WASSERMAN

BRIBED

The eminent Torah sage **RABBI ELCHONON WASSERMAN** (1875-1941), Rosh Yeshivah of Baranovitch, points out that although belief in God is self-evident to any rational thinker, many highly intelligent people are atheists or agnostics. How can this be? The answer, he says, is that they have been "bribed," which the Torah says has the power to mislead even a brilliant mind. What is the bribe that people accept to sway them from belief in Hashem? The desires of this world. When one wishes he could savor them and feels no guilt that he longs to disobey the Torah, he denies the existence of the Almighty.

"WE HUMANS RACE ACROSS THE WORLD TO DISCOVER THINGS… YET, ONE PLACE WE NEGLECT TO SEARCH IS OUR HEART… AND IT IS THERE THAT WE WILL FIND GOD."
— RABBI TZADOK HAKOHEN OF LUBLIN

It is so ironic. We launch the Hubble telescope to discover far-flung galaxies, and dispatch ocean explorers to solve the mysteries of the depths. Yet the secrets of our own essence — the depths of our hearts and the inner recesses of our souls — somehow remain uncharted! The profound thinker **RABBI TZADOK HAKOHEN** of Lublin (1823-1900) noted that were we to embark on a voyage within, we would find the greatest treasure in the world: faith in Hashem.

"FOR A PERSON WITH NO PARNASAH, IT'S CLEAR TO ME HOW HE LIVES — HE LIVES OFF EMUNAH AND BITACHON. BUT WHEN A PERSON HAS PARNASAH, HOW — IN FACT — DOES HE LIVE?"

— RABBI SIMCHA BUNIM OF PESHISCHA

The Chassidic master, **RABBI SIMCHA BUNIM OF PESHISCHA** (1765-1827), inspired Jews with his absolute faith and trust in the Creator. He *lived* with this emunah and bitachon; they sustained him. He wondered aloud how people with abundant livelihood live. It's one thing if one lives in constant need; his reliance on God creates an intimate, life-giving bond. But with financial independence from Hashem, asked the Peshischa Rebbe, can man truly live a connected life?

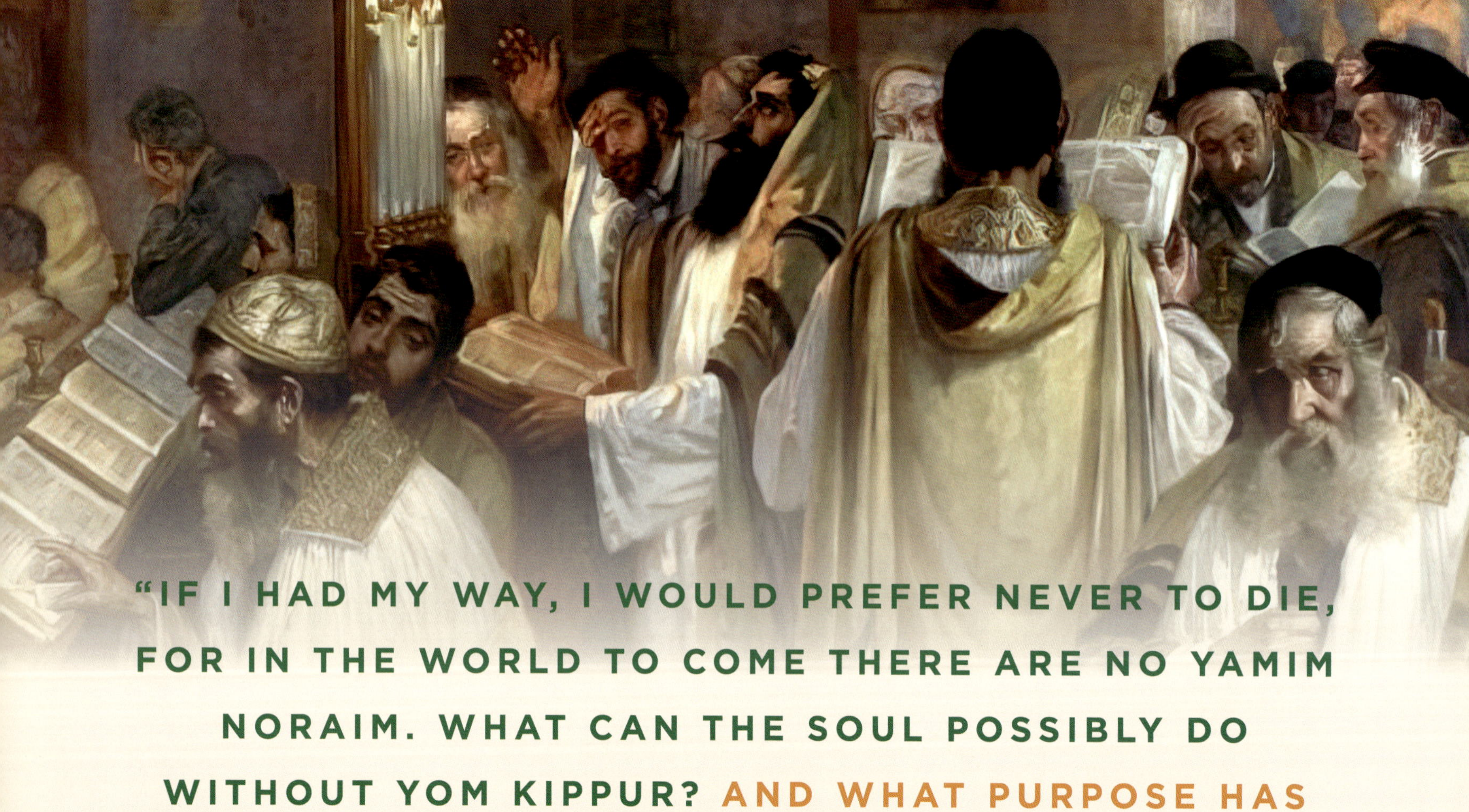
"IF I HAD MY WAY, I WOULD PREFER NEVER TO DIE, FOR IN THE WORLD TO COME THERE ARE NO YAMIM NORAIM. WHAT CAN THE SOUL POSSIBLY DO WITHOUT YOM KIPPUR? AND WHAT PURPOSE HAS LIFE WITHOUT TESHUVAH?"

— RABBI SHMELKA OF NIKOLSBURG

RETURN

We mortals so desire life, and so fear death. Each person has his or her own reasons for their attachment to this world. The reason given by the legendary *tzaddik* **RABBI SHMUEL SHMELKA HALEVI HOROWITZ** of Nikolsburg (1726-1778) is as fascinating as it is inspiring. He desired life because only this world features the awesome day of Yom Kippur with its restorative power of repentance. The singular opportunity for one's sullied soul to purify itself before God and sense, once again, His loving embrace is something one can savor in this world only. Who would want to take leave of such a sublime, magnificent place?

"IF IT COULD BE BETTER —
IT WOULD BE BETTER!"
— THE CHOFETZ CHAIM

SATISFACTION

Do not think that if something is not going well in life, it actually could be better. Hashem, in His infinite wisdom, determines what is truly best for each person, and allocates what one gets by what he truly needs. Hence, when someone complained to the Chofetz Chaim, **RABBI YISRAEL MEIR KAGAN** (1838-1933), that his situation "could be better," the saintly leader insisted that his mindset was flawed. No one wants the best for you more than Hashem. Hence, without a doubt, one's current situation is the best situation one can be in right now. If things could be better — then they would be better!

"WE PRAISE GOD FOR REDEEMING US FROM EGYPT NOT ONLY BROADLY, BUT EVEN FOR THE MINUTEST OF DETAILS — SUCH AS THE FACT THAT HE FREED US DURING THE DELIGHTFUL SPRINGTIME SEASON."
— THE ALTER OF SLABODKA

Hakaras hatov, feeling and acknowledging the good that others have granted us, is something we should strive to achieve both with Hashem and with our fellow man. But a general statement of thanks does not suffice. We owe those who have helped us an itemized list of appreciation, detailing each and every facet that was involved in their efforts on our behalf. The Alter of Slabodka, **RABBI NOSSON TZVI FINKEL** (1849-1927), brings a proof to this from the Torah. Regarding the Exodus, Moshe tells the Jewish people, "Today you are leaving, in the month of springtime" (*Shemos* 13:4). Rashi explains that he was saying, "See the kindness that God has bestowed on you: He brought you forth in a month that is fit for going out — neither hot nor cold nor rainy." Although the Jewish people would have been elated to leave Egypt regardless of the climate, it is incumbent upon us, as beneficiaries of Hashem's kindness, to take note of the wonderful weather in which we left. This is the extent we must go to when showing gratitude to others.

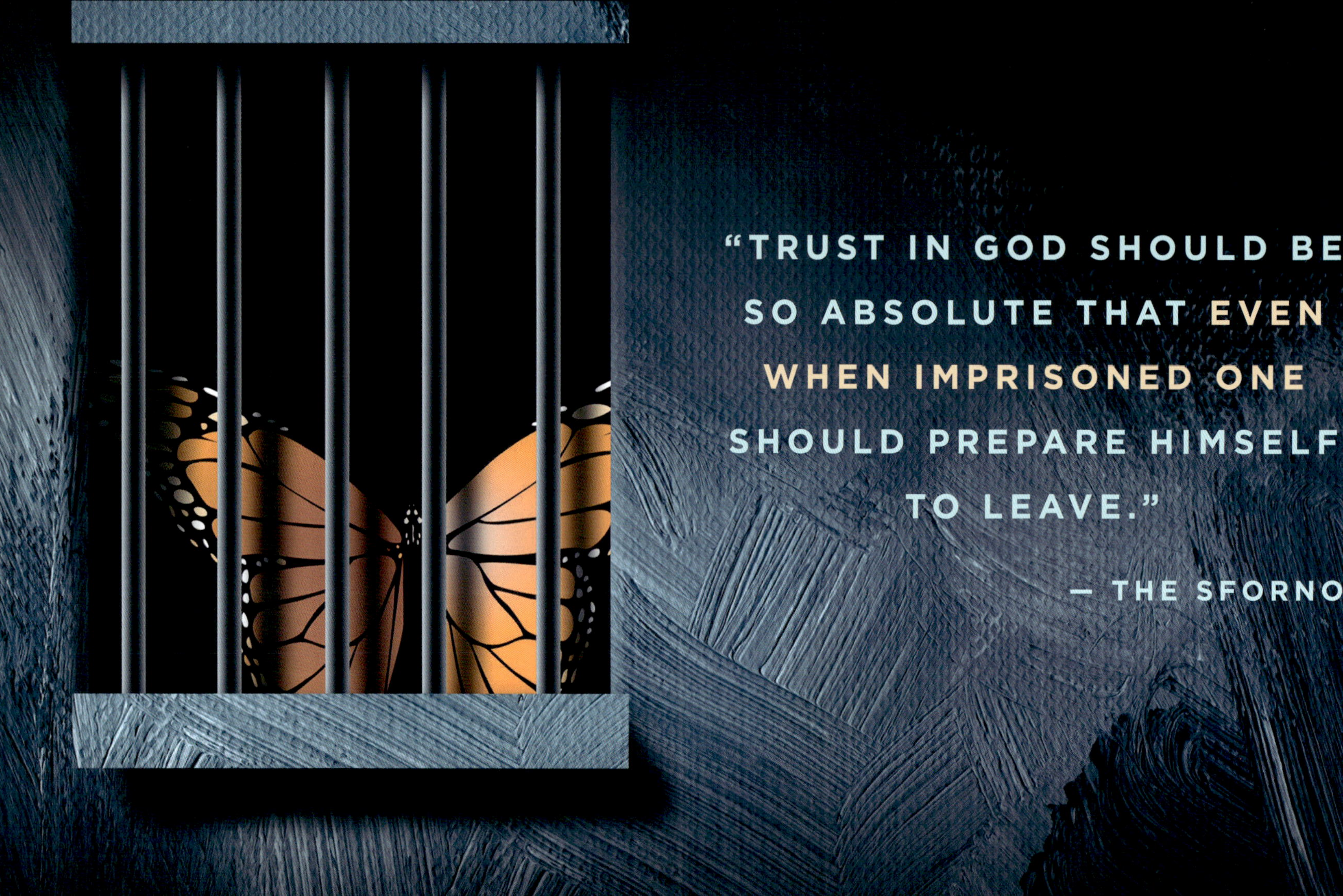

"TRUST IN GOD SHOULD BE SO ABSOLUTE THAT EVEN WHEN IMPRISONED ONE SHOULD PREPARE HIMSELF TO LEAVE."
— THE SFORNO

The major Torah commentary entitled *Sforno*, written by **RABBEINU OVADIA SFORNO** (c. 1475-1550), notes that the Jews, on the night of the Exodus from Egyptian slavery, were to eat their Korban Pesach, "belts tightened, shoes on feet, and staff in hand" (*Shemos* 12:11). This shows that they fully believed in God's imminent redemption. The Mashgiach of the Mir Yeshivah, Rabbi Yerucham Levovitz (1873-1936), adds that the Sforno's concept reflects the core concept of mitzvos and their promised reward. We perform them in this world (akin to a prison), preparing ourselves for our reward in the Coming World.

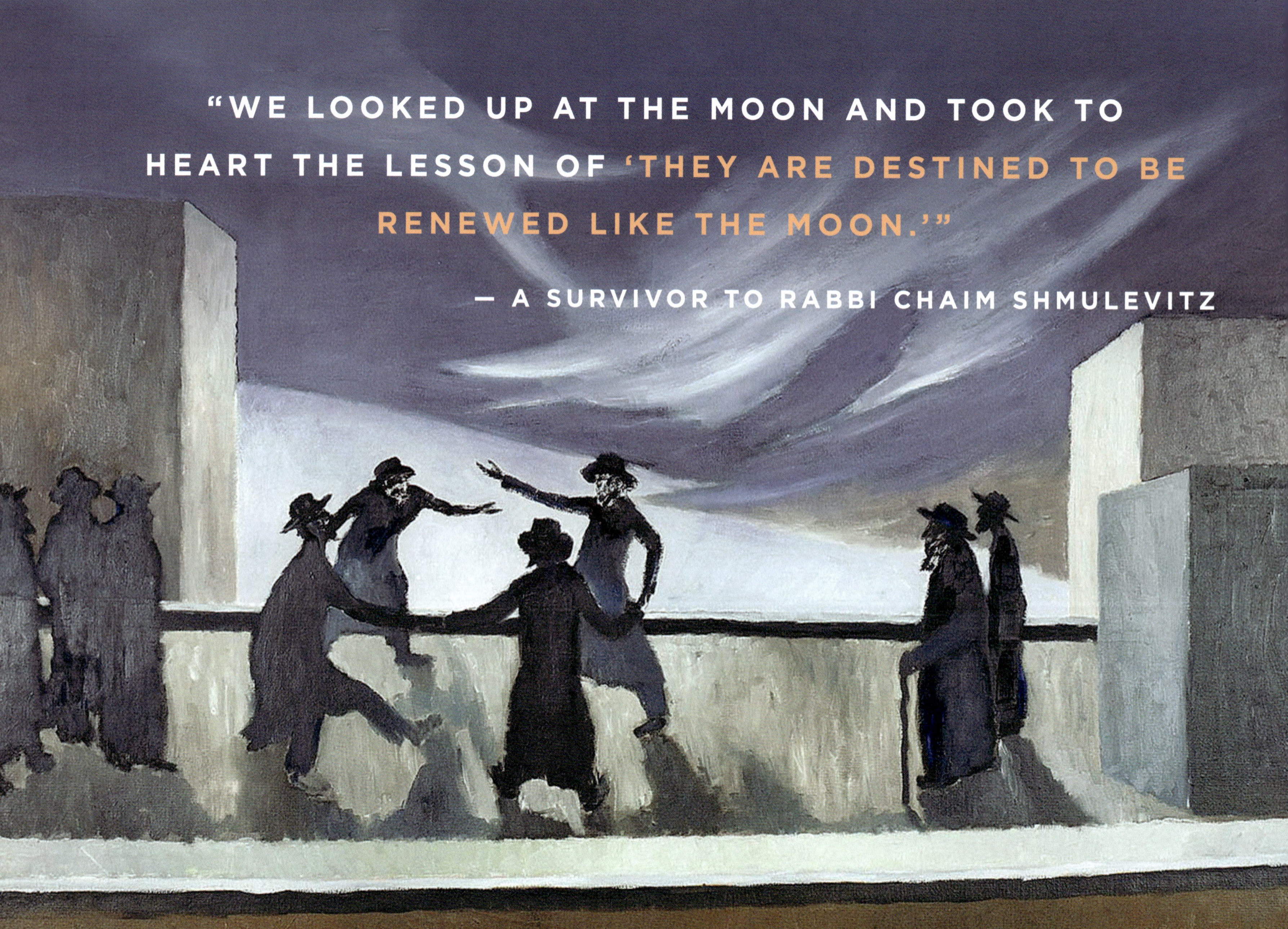

"WE LOOKED UP AT THE MOON AND TOOK TO HEART THE LESSON OF 'THEY ARE DESTINED TO BE RENEWED LIKE THE MOON.'"
— A SURVIVOR TO RABBI CHAIM SHMULEVITZ

DESTINY

RABBI CHAIM SHMULEVITZ (1902-1979), Rosh Yeshivah of Mir, once met a Holocaust survivor and asked him, "How did you hold out? How was it you were able to not give up?" The Jew told Rav Chaim that in the camps, they could not fulfill most mitzvos. However, they performed one mitzvah regularly. Even at the risk of death, they left the barracks at night to fulfill the mitzvah of *Kiddush Levanah*. There was always a moon. "We looked up at the moon and we took to heart the lesson of 'they are destined to be renewed like the moon.'" This is what gave this Jew hope...

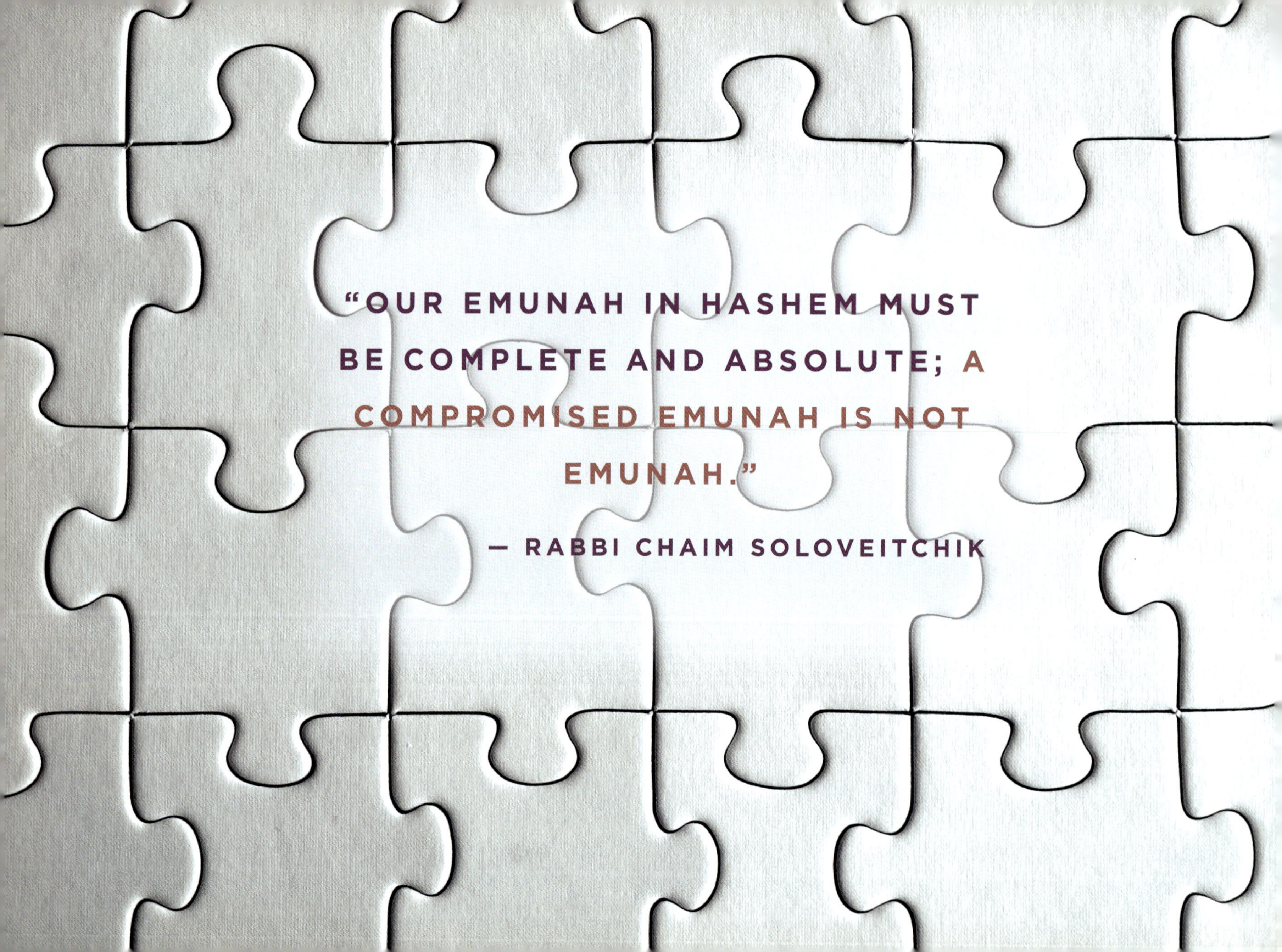

"OUR EMUNAH IN HASHEM MUST BE COMPLETE AND ABSOLUTE; A COMPROMISED EMUNAH IS NOT EMUNAH."
— RABBI CHAIM SOLOVEITCHIK

In *Sefer Melachim* (I, 18:21), we find that Eliyahu HaNavi tells the Jewish people who assembled at Har HaCarmel, "Until when are you hopping between two ideas? If you want to follow Hashem, choose His way. If you want to follow the Ba'al, then follow him." **RABBI CHAIM SOLOVEITCHIK** (1853-1918) of Brisk asked, "If someone eats both kosher and non-kosher food, we don't give him an ultimatum that if he continues to eat *treif*, he should not eat kosher. Why, then, did Eliyahu tell the people to choose one way or the other?" Rav Chaim answered that when it comes to matters of emunah and bitachon, one cannot fluctuate between truth and untruth, as absolutely no compromise is permitted.

"THIS IS A PREVIEW OF MASHIACH'S TIMES, WHEN HASHEM WILL GATHER THE JEWS FROM ALL PARTS OF THE WORLD AND FLY THEM OVER THE OCEANS TO ERETZ YISRAEL, AS IT SAYS (SHEMOS 19:4), 'I LIFTED THEM ON EAGLE'S WINGS...'"

— REB YAAKOV YOSEF HERMAN

Gedolim have an uncanny ability to view stories in the news through the prism of Torah, understanding the essential messages that must be taken from current events. An example of this is **REB YAAKOV YOSEF HERMAN** (1880-1967), an American Torah pioneer who planted holy seeds into the then-arid soil of the United States. When Charles Lindbergh embarked on the first non-stop solo flight from New York to Paris, the world anxiously awaited news of this historic event. Reb Yaakov Yosef ran into his house waving the newspaper with the glaring headline hailing his successful landing in Paris. "He made it!" Reb Yaakov Yosef said. He then sat down in his chair and absorbed the significance of this for the Jewish people. It was not merely a great aeronautical achievement, but it reinforced his emunah in the masterplan of Mashiach's arrival, seeing the airplane as the vehicle through which the ingathering of the Jewish people from *galus* will be carried out.

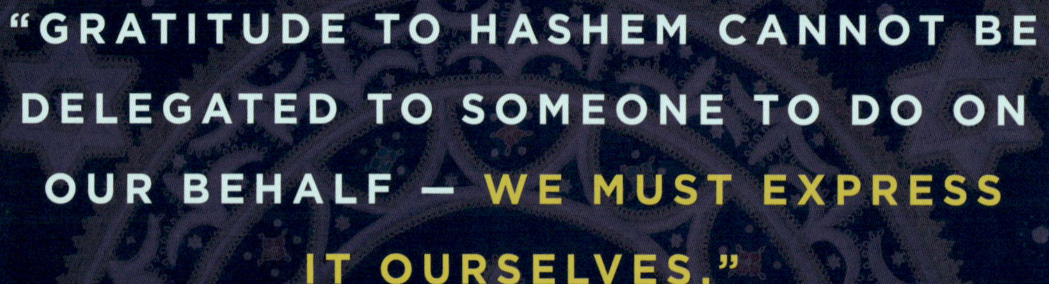
"GRATITUDE TO HASHEM CANNOT BE DELEGATED TO SOMEONE TO DO ON OUR BEHALF — WE MUST EXPRESS IT OURSELVES."

— THE ABUDRAHAM

מודים

אנחנו לך שאתה הוא אלקינו

ואלקי אבותינו אלקי כל בשר

When the *chazzan* reaches *Modim* (Thanksgiving) in his repetition of *Shemoneh Esrei* (*Chazaras Hashatz*), all the people present recite their own *Modim* (*D'Rabbanan*) prayer, rather than merely listening to the *chazzan* (as they do the rest of *Chazaras Hashatz*). **RABBEINU DAVID ABUDRAHAM** (14th century), author of the seminal work on prayer, explains the reason behind this. Just as a servant does not thank his master through a messenger, for gratitude is not something to be delegated to others, we, too, must thank God individually, and cannot fulfill our obligation of *Modim* by means of the efforts of the *chazzan*.

> **"EMUNAH IS THE HEART OF THE SPIRITUAL BODY, PUMPING LIFE INTO ALL THE OTHER MITZVOS."**
>
> **— THE MAHARSHA**

Sign on a field in Israel, declaring that Shemittah is observed on it

VITALITY

The Gemara in *Makkos* (23b-24b) says that Moshe Rabbeinu was given 613 mitzvos on Har Sinai... consisting of 248 positive mitzvos corresponding to the number of organs in a person's body... Chabakuk came and summarized them all in one, "A *tzaddik* lives through his emunah" (*Chabakuk* 2:4). The Maharsha, **RABBI SHMUEL EIDELS** (1555-1631), explains that emunah in Hashem is so fundamental that it is the summation of all the mitzvos of the Torah. He likens faith to the heart of the spiritual body. Just as the 248 organs of the human body are energized by the heart, so are all the 248 positive mitzvos — corresponding to the number of organs — infused with purpose and connection to the Divine through emunah. [A classic example of this is the mitzvah of Shemittah, requiring the farmer in Israel to let his land — and primary source of income — lie fallow every seventh year, a supreme act of faith.]

"A FRIGHTENING CLAP OF THUNDER
PRECEDES A DOWNPOUR OF RAIN.
TO BRING BLESSING, WE MUST FIRST
BE STIRRED TO REPENT."

– RABBI ELYAH LOPIAN

AWAKEN

A shower of rain often follows a heavy barrage of thunder and lightning. To explain this series of events, the great Mussar personality **RABBI ELYAH LOPIAN** (1876-1970) conveys the following: Hashem, in His infinite kindness, wants to send His blessed rain down to earth. When He sees, though, that we do not have sufficient merit to warrant this, He unleashes a thunderstorm to startle us, arousing us to repent before Him (see *Berachos* 59a). Once that occurs, we are deemed worthy of receiving the rain, and it gushes down. Hashem operates this way in general. He, at times, sends us shocking news, hoping to instill a fear of Heaven into us, thereby paving the way for us to be the beneficiaries of goodness from on high.

"TO LIVE WITHOUT DEPENDENCE ON GOD — THIS
IS THE ULTIMATE CURSE."

— RABBI SIMCHA BUNIM OF PESHISCHA

At the start of *Sefer Bereishis* (3:14), God punished the snake for instigating the original sin by decreeing, "The dust of the earth you shall eat all the days of your life." The Chassidic leader, **RABBI SIMCHA BUNIM OF PESHISCHA** (1765-1827), asks why this is considered a punishment. After all, dirt is ubiquitous; the snake would never have to work to obtain sustenance! The answer he gives is spectacular. God wants us to pray and ask Him for help when we need it, for by doing so a close bond is formed between Him and us. The snake, while fortunate to have a constant diet of dirt, has nothing to ask of God. This, says Rav Simcha Bunim, is the supreme curse, for living independently of God deprives one of forming a meaningful relationship with Him.

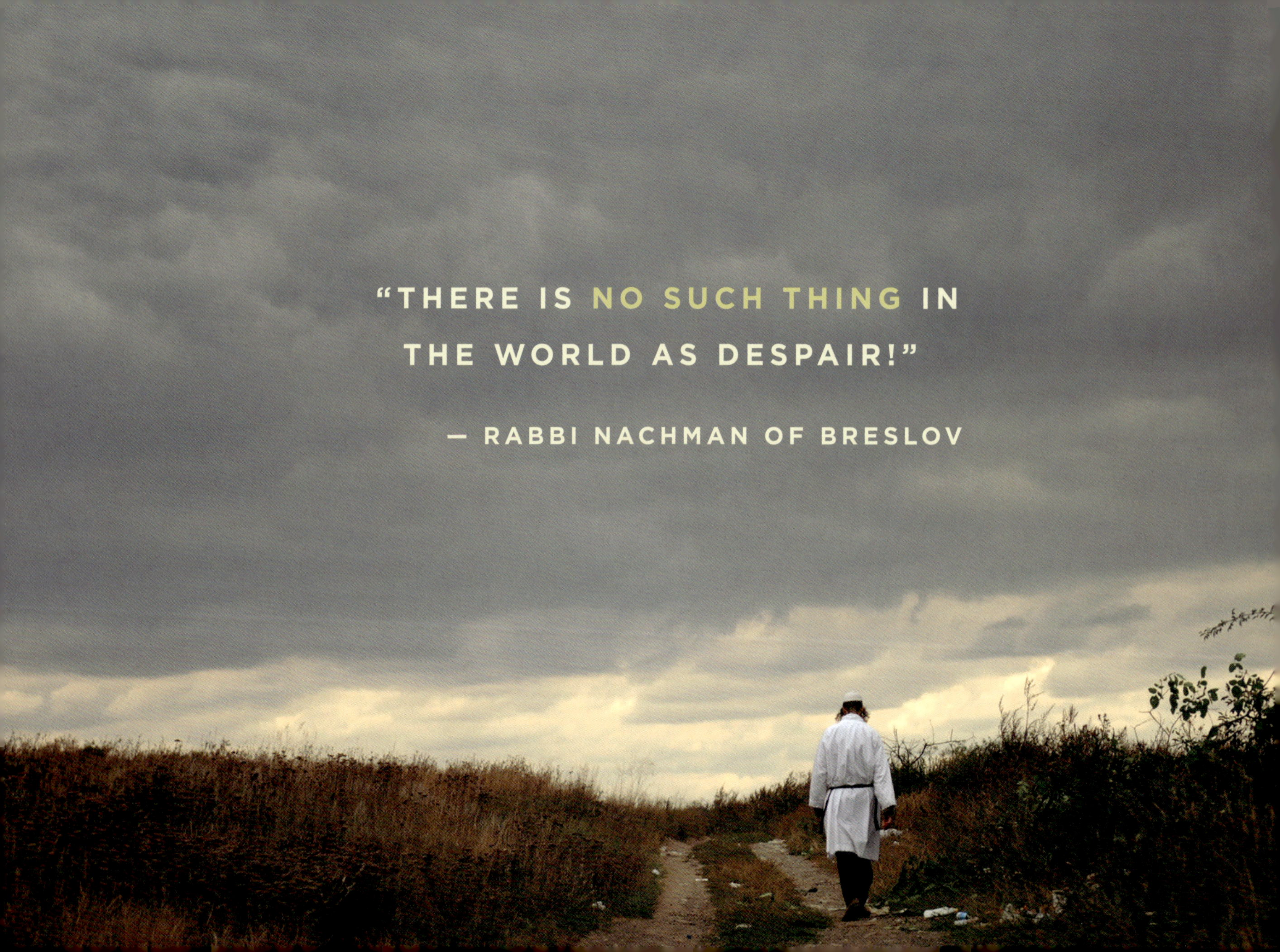

"THERE IS NO SUCH THING IN THE WORLD AS DESPAIR!"

— RABBI NACHMAN OF BRESLOV

When the celebrated Chassidic master **RABBI NACHMAN OF BRESLOV** (1772-1810) shared these words with his followers, he expressed them emphatically and with awesome depth, in order to convey to each person, throughout the generations, never to despair under any circumstances, no matter what. He instructed that even if one has fallen to the lowest of places, God forbid, he can still repent and return to God. These words have soothed the hearts of many since Rav Nachman first uttered them, as they reignite an inner passion for Hashem and restore faith in ourselves.

"A HEDGE OF ROSES IS A DETERRENT ONLY TO ONE WHOSE LOVE OF ROSES WOULD NOT PERMIT HIM TO TRAMPLE ON THEIR BEAUTY; A JEW WILL NOT VIOLATE SHABBOS BECAUSE OF THE SHEER LOVE HE HAS FOR IT."

— RABBI MORDECHAI GIFTER

In *Zemiros*, the Shabbos is described as being *fenced in by roses,* which means that the Jewish people are praised for willingly allowing themselves to be restricted and "fenced in" by the laws of the Torah, called a *hedge of roses* (*Shir HaShirim* 7:3). **RABBI MORDECHAI GIFTER** (1915-2001), Rosh Yeshivah of Telshe, explains this description as follows. A fence made up of roses alone cannot stop a person from trespassing, as it can be easily trampled upon. Its deterrent power is based on the belief that someone who loves roses would never destroy their beauty by crushing their hedges. Likewise, a Torah observant Jew, although not physically prevented from desecrating the Shabbos, would never permit himself to violate its laws due to his innate love for Shabbos.

"THE THIRD BEIS HAMIKDASH WILL BE BUILT BY MAN, BUT — LIKE A SOUL ENTERING A BODY — A SPIRITUAL EDIFICE WILL DESCEND FROM HEAVEN, IMBUING THE TEMPLE WITH ITS SANCTITY."

— RABBI YAAKOV ETTLINGER

PERMEATE

Although there are conflicting opinions regarding who will construct the Third Holy Temple — whether God or the Jewish people — the *Aruch LaNer*, **RABBI YAAKOV ETTLINGER** (1798-1871) of Altona, suggests a compromise. The future Beis HaMikdash, he submits, will be man-made. Those sources that maintain that it will descend from Heaven refer to the *spiritual edifice* that will come down and infuse the earthly one with its sanctity, much like a soul entering the body of a person.

"WHEN YOU ARE TRAVELING AND CANNOT STUDY AND PRAY AS USUAL, DO NOT BE DISTRESSED. GOD WANTS YOU TO WORSHIP HIM IN DIFFERENT WAYS..."
— THE BAAL SHEM TOV

There are many times that life does not go exactly as planned, and we find ourselves far from the comfort of home as we travel on a journey far away. We miss our daily regimen of davening and learning, and we long for our family and friends. The **BAAL SHEM TOV** (1698-1760), founder of Chassidus, cautions us to stay positive and strong, armed with the faith that whatever happens is for a Divine purpose. Although the new terrain may be unfamiliar, Hashem is a constant; He is always with us. Utilize this circumstance to discover new ways to serve Him.

"'YEHUDIM' (JEWS) SHARES THE SAME NUMERICAL VALUE (75) AS THE WORD 'BITACHON.' INDEED, A JEW LIVES — AND IS DEFINED — BY HIS CONSTANT BITACHON."

— THE BEN ISH CHAI

EQUIVALENCE

RABBI YOSEF CHAIM (1835-1909), the celebrated Ben Ish Chai, was one of Sephardic Jewry's greatest luminaries. In an address he delivered on Shabbos Zachor, to an overflow crowd in his large shul in Baghdad, he spoke of the bitachon demonstrated by the Jews in the time of Purim. He notes that the *gematria*, numerical value, of *Yehudim* and *bitachon* is the same — 75 — and explains that they are truly the same, for the Jewish people always place their trust in God. It is for this reason, the Ben Ish Chai continued, that the Megillah refers to the Jews by the name *Yehudim*, because in the era of Purim, although the Jews were not perfect, they maintained their bitachon in Hashem, and for that reason they merited their miraculous salvation.

"THE FOLLOWING BLESSINGS ARE TO BE RECITED
WHEN MASHIACH ARRIVES…"

— RABBI SHLOMO ZALMAN AUERBACH

Personal pen of Rabbi
Shlomo Zalman Auerbach

IMMINENT

RABBI SHLOMO ZALMAN AUERBACH (1910-1995), revered and beloved Rosh Yeshivah of Kol Torah and a leading halachic authority of his time, discusses in a responsum what blessings should be recited upon the arrival of Mashiach.

He rules that four *berachos* should be said:

- חכם הרזים, the *berachah* you make when seeing 600,000 Jews, because certainly there will be at least that many that accompany the Melech HaMashiach.
- שחלק מחכמתו ליראיו, the *berachah* upon seeing a wise man.
- שחלק מכבודו ליראיו, the *berachah* upon seeing a king.
- שהחיינו, Shehecheyanu.

This letter fills the reader with excitement to prepare for Mashiach's imminent arrival...

HASHGACHAH PRATIS JOURNAL

In a public letter issued in 1984, the two towering Torah leaders, Rabbi Moshe Feinstein (1895-1986) and Rabbi Yaakov Kamenetsky (1891-1986), wrote the following: "Any thoughtful person understands the importance in our times of implanting emunah and *Hashgachah Pratis*. This is especially critical when educating our youth, because this pillar upholds our entire belief system. A good strategy for reinforcing this faith is to keep a notebook chronicling any situation in which a person sees and feels Hashem's *Hashgachah Pratis* in matters of daily life. Doing this will certainly uproot and negate the sense that things occur at random, that forces of nature control our lives, or that, 'It is the power of my hand' that accomplishes things in life…"

TODAY'S DATE __/__/__

____

____

____

____

____

____

____

____

____

TODAY'S DATE __/__/__

____

____

____

____

____

____

____

____

____

HASHGACHAH PRATIS JOURNAL

TODAY'S DATE __/__/__

TODAY'S DATE __/__/__

HASHGACHAH PRATIS JOURNAL

TODAY'S DATE __/__/__

TODAY'S DATE __/__/__

HASHGACHAH PRATIS JOURNAL

TODAY'S DATE __/__/__

TODAY'S DATE __/__/__

HASHGACHAH PRATIS JOURNAL

TODAY'S DATE __/__/__

TODAY'S DATE __/__/__

HASHGACHAH PRATIS JOURNAL

TODAY'S DATE __/__/__

TODAY'S DATE __/__/__

TODAY'S DATE __/__/__

TODAY'S DATE __/__/__

TODAY'S DATE __/__/__

TODAY'S DATE __/__/__

TODAY'S DATE __/__/__

TODAY'S DATE __/__/__

HASHGACHAH PRATIS JOURNAL

TODAY'S DATE __/__/__

TODAY'S DATE __/__/__

HASHGACHAH PRATIS JOURNAL

TODAY'S DATE __/__/__

____

____

____

____

____

____

____

____

____

TODAY'S DATE __/__/__

____

____

____

____

____

____

____

____

____

HASHGACHAH PRATIS JOURNAL

TODAY'S DATE __/__/__

TODAY'S DATE __/__/__

HASHGACHAH PRATIS JOURNAL

TODAY'S DATE __/__/__

TODAY'S DATE __/__/__

HASHGACHAH PRATIS JOURNAL

TODAY'S DATE __/__/__

TODAY'S DATE __/__/__

TODAY'S DATE __/__/__

TODAY'S DATE __/__/__

TODAY'S DATE __/__/__

TODAY'S DATE __/__/__

HASHGACHAH PRATIS JOURNAL

TODAY'S DATE __/__/__

TODAY'S DATE __/__/__

TODAY'S DATE __/__/__

TODAY'S DATE __/__/__

TODAY'S DATE __/__/__

TODAY'S DATE __/__/__

TODAY'S DATE __/__/__

TODAY'S DATE __/__/__

HASHGACHAH PRATIS JOURNAL

TODAY'S DATE __/__/__

TODAY'S DATE __/__/__

HASHGACHAH PRATIS JOURNAL

TODAY'S DATE __/__/__

TODAY'S DATE __/__/__

TODAY'S DATE __/__/__

TODAY'S DATE __/__/__

HASHGACHAH PRATIS JOURNAL

TODAY'S DATE __/__/__

TODAY'S DATE __/__/__

TODAY'S DATE __/__/__

TODAY'S DATE __/__/__

GLOSSARY

Alter – the Elder; a title of reverence for a great sage
Aron Kodesh – Holy Torah Ark
Bachur – unmarried yeshivah student
Bar Mitzvah – one to whom the commandments apply; when a Jewish boy reaches the age of thirteen
Baruch Hashem – Thank God!
Beis HaMikdash – the Holy Temple in Jerusalem
Beis Medrash – study hall
Bitachon – trust in God
Chassid – pious individual
Chassidus – Chassidic movement
Chazzan – cantor; leader of prayers
Chessed – kindness
Daven – pray
Emunah – faith in God
Eretz Yisrael – the Land of Israel
Erev – the Eve of
Galus – exile, diaspora
Gaon – pride; brilliant Torah scholar
Gedolei Yisrael/Gedolim – Torah giants
Gemara – Talmud
HaKadosh Baruch Hu – The Holy One, Blessed is He; God
Halachah (pl. Halachos) – Torah Law
Hashem – God
Hashgachah Pratis – Divine Providence
Kiddush Hashem – sanctification of God's Name

Kiddush Levanah – sanctifying the new moon
Kohen – a descendant of the ancient priestly class
Korban Pesach – Pesach offering
Krias Shema – recitation of the Shema prayer, in which we accept God's absolute sovereignty
Mashgiach [Ruchani] – spiritual advisor in a yeshivah who is a mentor to the students
Megillah or Megillas Esther – Book (or Scroll) of Esther
Mesorah – tradition
Mitzvah (pl. Mitzvos) – commandment
Mashiach – Messiah
Mussar – Jewish ethics and moral teachings
Rabbeinu – grand title for our rabbinic teachers
Rabbanim — rabbis
Rambam – Rabbi **M**oshe **B**en **M**aimon (1135-1204)
Ramban – Rabbi **M**oshe **B**en **N**achman (1194-1270)
Rashi – Rabbi **S**hlomo **Y**itzchaki (1040-1105)
Rav — Rabbi
Rebbe – Torah mentor or Chassidic leader
Ribbono Shel Olam – Master of the Universe
Rosh Yeshivah (pl. Roshei Yeshivah) – Dean of a Yeshivah
Sefer (pl. Sefarim) – book
Sefer Torah (pl. Sifrei Torah) – Torah scroll
Sepharadi (pl. Sepharadim) – the Jews of Spain, Portugal, North Africa and the Middle East and their descendants

Shabbos – Sabbath

Shema – prayer in which we accept God's absolute sovereignty

Shiur (pl. Shiurim) – Torah lecture

Shul – synagogue

Shulchan Aruch – Code of Jewish Law

Siddur (pl. Siddurim) – Prayer book

Talmid (pl. Talmidim) – student

Tefillah – prayer

Tehillim – Psalms

Teshuvah – repentance

Tzaddik (pl. Tzaddikim) – righteous person

Yeshivah (pl. Yeshivos) – Torah academy

Yetzer Hara — the evil inclination

Yom Tov – Festival

Yamim Noraim — the High Holidays

Z"L — abbreviation of **Z**ichrono **L**ivrachah, May his memory be for a blessing

SOURCES

Note: The quotations contained in this book often have different versions and are sometimes attributed to more than one Torah personality. Additionally, the translations have often been modified by the author in order to convey the message vividly and succinctly.

M.B.

Page 16   The Chofetz Chaim's *Nefutzos Yisrael,* ch. 7.
Page 18   *B'Mechitzasam,* Vol. II, by Rabbi Shlomo Lorincz, Feldheim Publishers, pp. 660.
Page 20   *HaRav HaDomeh L'Malach*, by Rabbi C.S. Rosental, p. 76.
Page 22   Rabbi Eliyahu Lopian is cited in several sources as having heard from the Alter of Kelm.
Page 24   *Rav Chaim Kanievsky Haggadah*, by Rabbi Avraham Yeshayahu Shteinman, Mesorah Publications, pp. 126-128.
Page 26   *The Torah Profile*, article on the Skulener Rebbe by Rabbi Nisson Wolpin, Mesorah Publications, p. 273; *Around the Maggid's Table*, by Rabbi Paysach J. Krohn, Mesorah Publications, pp. 242-244.
Page 28   Rabbi Shlomo Wolbe's *B'emunaso Yichyeh,* p. 120.
Page 30   *Rabbi Avigdor Miller, His Life and Revolution*, by Rabbi Yaakov Y. Hamburger and Rabbi Yaakov Astor, Judaica Press, p. 273.
Page 32   *Mesillas Yesharim*, ch. 1.
Page 34   Rabbi Samson Raphael Hirsch's commentary to *Shemos* 34:7.
Page 36   *Rav Pam*, by Rabbi Shimon Finkelman, Mesorah Publications, pp. 391-394.
Page 38   Rabbeinu Yonah's *Shaarei Teshuvah* (2:5); Rav Hutner addition from *Ohel Moshe*, by Rabbi Moshe Scheinerman, *Vayikra*, p. 336.
Page 40   Rabbi Chaim Shmulevitz's *Sichos Mussar* (5733), p. 73.
Page 42   *B'Mechitzasam,* Vol. II, by Rabbi Shlomo Lorincz, Feldheim Publishers, p. 578; *The Rosh Yeshivah Remembers*, by Rabbi Asher Bergman, Mesorah Publications, pp. 304-305.

Page 44   Disseminated as final KAJ Speech; cf. *Rav Schwab on Prayer*, p. 5.

Page 46   Chazon Ish's *Emunah U'Bitachon* 2:2; see Rabbi Moshe Aharon Stern's *Bayis U'Menucha*, p. 110.

Page 48   *Ibn Ezra* to *Shemos* 20:13.

Page 50   Chasam Sofer's *Derashos,* p. 127.

Page 52   *Mishpacha Magazine*, Sept. 18, 2019, "Sharing the Wealth," by Rabbi Eliyahu Gut and Rabbi Ephraim Zalman Galinsky.

Page 54   *Shaarei Orah* (*Sichos* of Rav Avigdor Miller), Vol. 1, p. 148.

Page 56   *Shelah* (*Parashas B'haaloscha, Derech Chaim Tochachas Mussar* 12); cf. Rabbeinu Yonah to *Mishlei* 3:6; see Rabbi Moshe Aharon Stern's *Bayis U'Menucha,* p. 108.

Page 58   *A Tzaddik in Our Time*, by Rabbi Simcha Raz, Feldheim Publishers, p. 420.

Page 60   Widely quoted.

Page 62   Rabbi Shach's *Avi Ezri, Hilchos Teshuvah* 5:5.

Page 64   Rambam's *Peirush HaMishnayos* to *Berachos,* ch. 9.

Page 66   *Jewish Observer,* Jan. 1990, p. 8, article by Rabbi Shimon Finkelman.

Page 68   *Orchos Chaim LeHaRosh*, #26.

Page 70   Rabbi Ovadia Yosef's *Anaf Eitz Avos*, *Avos* 2:13.

Page 72   Rabbi Chaim Shmulevitz's *Sichos Mussar, Shaarei Chaim, maamar* 16.

Page 74   *Yalkut Me'am Lo'ez, Sefer Shoftim,* p. 81.

Page 76   Beis HaLevi's *Maamar HaBitachon,* ch. 11.

Page 78   *Avnei Shlomo*, p. 103; see *Rabbi Avigdor Miller — His Life and His Revolution*, p. 276, where a similar story is told about Rabbi Levi Yitzchak of Berditchev.

Page 80   *Otzros Meforshei HaTefillah*, by Rabbi Shimon Vanunu, p. 440.

Page 82   *Chidushei Maran Riz HaLevi al HaTorah, Parashas Bereishis; A Golden Bridge* (Mir Yeshivah), p. 125.

Page 84   *Mishpacha Magazine*, April 22, 2020, article on the Novominsker Rebbe, *All on His Shoulders*, by Rabbi Yisroel Besser.

Page 86   Rabbi Yerucham Levovitz's *Daas Chochmah U'Mussar* (Vol. II *maamar* 29); *Maamar Mordechai,* by Rabbi Mordechai Schwab, Vol. II, p. 172, fn.

Page 88   Rabbi Levovitz's *Daas Torah, Parashas Lech Lecha,* p. 156; cf. *Parashas Shoftim,* pp. 237-240.

Page 90   Cited by Rabbi Chaim Brim in *Marbeh Chaim.*

Page 92   Vilna Gaon's commentary to *Mishlei* 22:19.

Page 94   *Yated Ne'eman*, May 13, 2022, article by Rabbi Pinchos Lipschutz, p. 61.

Page 96   Rabbeinu Yonah's *Shaarei Teshuvah* 3:32; see *Derech Sichah* (comments of Rabbi Chaim Kanievsky), p. 8.

Page 98 ArtScroll's *Shaar HaBitachon*, p. 32, fn.

Page 100 *Chofetz Chaim al HaTorah, Parashas VaEschanan, Maasai LaMelech,* p. 230

Page 102 Rabbi Dessler's *Michtav MeEliyahu,* Vol. III, p. 176; cf. *Talilei Oros,* preface to *Parashas Bereishis,* p. 15.

Page 104 A *Treasury of Chassidic Tales,* by Rabbi Shlomo Yosef Zevin, Mesorah Publications, p. 142.

Page 106 Rabbi Abba Shaul's *Ohr LeTzion — Chochmah U'Mussar,* p. 142.

Page 108 *Beis HaLevi, Parashas Beshalach.*

Page 110 *Rabbi Yisrael Salanter: Chayav, Pe'ulosav, v'Talmidav,* by Rabbi Shmuel Rosenfeld, p. 38.

Page 112 *The Manchester Rosh Yeshivah,* by Rabbi Shimon Finkelman with Rabbi Yosef Weiss, Mesorah Publications, p. 360.

Page 114 *A Living Mishnas Rav Aharon,* by Rabbi Yitzchok Dershowitz, Feldheim Publishers, pp. 174-175; *Imrei Mordechai* (Rabbi Mordechai Shapiro), pp. 142-143.

Page 116 *Nefesh HaChaim* 3:12; *Rabboseinu,* p. 170.

Page 118 *Chofetz Chaim al HaTorah,* p. 69, in *Maasai LaMelech.*

Page 120 *Meshech Chochmah, Devarim* 10:20.

Page 122 *Igros Moshe, Yoreh De'ah II,* #76; *Reb Moshe* (25th Anniversary edition), by Rabbi Shimon Finkelman, Mesorah Publications, p. 383.

Page 124 *Sefer HaChinuch,* 241.

Page 126 Rabbi Samson Raphael Hirsch's commentary to *Tehillim* (22:2) and *Shemos* (32:11).

Page 128 *Likutei Torah, Parashas Re'eh.*

Page 130 *Toras Avos,* תשכ״א-תשס״ט, p. 149.

Page 132 See Steipler Gaon's *Chayei Olam,* ch. 28; *A Letter for the Ages,* by Rabbi Avrohom Chaim Feuer, Mesorah Publications, pp. 120-121.

Page 134 *Chofetz Chaim al HaTorah, to Bereishis* 8:22; addition regarding Mashiach, from *Ohel Moshe* (Bereishis, p. 144).

Page 136 *Bnei Yissaschar, Maamarei Chodesh Sivan,* 5:2, p. 71.

Page 138 Rabbi Abba Shaul's *Ohr LeTzion — Chochmah U'Mussar,* pp. 70-71.

Page 140 *Pachad Yitzchak, Pesach, maamar* 14.

Page 142 *HaMeoros HaGedolim,* by Rabbi Chaim Ephraim Zaitchik, p. 208.

Page 144 *Rabbi Yisrael Baal Shem Tov,* by Eliezer Steinman, p. 89.

Page 146 Introduction to *Sefer Aish Kodesh,* by Rabbi Ahron Surasky, p. 13; cf. *Great Jewish Letters,* p. 80.

Page 148 *Yalkut Lekach Tov, Shemos,* p. 258.

Page 150 *The Zemiros Treasury,* Feldheim Publishers, p. 81.

Page 152 Chazon Ish's *Emunah U'Bitachon,* ch. 2; see ArtScroll's *Shaar HaBitachon,* p. 23, fn.

Page 154 Ramban's *HaEmunah VeHaBitachon,* ch. 1.

Page 156 *Sparks of Mussar*, by Rabbi Chaim Ephraim Zaitchik, chapter about Rabbi Hurwitz.

Page 158 *Haggadah Al Matzos Umerorim,* p. 111; *B'Mechitzasam*, by Rabbi Shlomo Lorincz, Feldheim Publishers, Vol. II, p. 352.

Page 160 See *Keser Shem Tov* (1999 ed.) in addendum, #67.

Page 162 Introduction to Rabbi Shkop's *Shaarei Yosher.*

Page 164 *Gedolei HaDoros*, by Rabbi Moshe Aharon Stern, p. 941.

Page 166 *Siach Sarfei Kodesh* 21:406; *Haggadah Chassidim Mesaprim*, p. 128.

Page 168 Rabbi Levenstein's *Ohr Yechezkel-Emunah*, p. 218.

Page 170 See ArtScroll's *Shaar HaBitachon*, p. 29, fn.

Page 172 Widely quoted.

Page 174 Quoted by Arizal's primary student, Rabbi Chaim Vital, in *Shaar HaGilgulim,* p. 62b.

Page 176 Rabbi Wasserman's *Kovetz He'aros, Dugmaos LeBiurei Aggados,* ch. 1; reprinted in new edition of *Kovetz Maamarim*, ch. 1.

Page 178 *Hasidic Wisdom*, by Rabbi Simcha Raz, p. 6.

Page 180 *Chassidim Mesaprim*, by Rabbi Yehudah Leib Levin, ch. 11:6.

Page 182 *Yom Kippur*, by Rabbi Nosson Scherman, Mesorah Publications, p. 55.

Page 184 *Chofetz Chaim al HaTorah, Parashas Ha'azinu, Maasai LaMelech*, 1.

Page 186 *Shaarei Orah*, by Rabbi Avigdor Miller, Vol. 1, p. 131-132.

Page 188 *Sforno* to Shemos 12:11: Rabbi Levovitz's *Daas Chochmah U'Mussar*, Vol. 6:1.

Page 190 Rabbi Yissachar Frand, Torah.org, *Parashas Bo.*

Page 192 *Rav Aharon Leib*, by Naftali Weinberger, Mesorah Publications, p. 52; *Yalkut Lekach Tov, Shemos*, p. 135.

Page 194 *All for the Boss*, by Ruchoma Shain, Feldheim Publishers, p. 27.

Page 196 *Abudraham, Seder Shacharis shel Chol U'Peirushah.*

Page 198 *Maharsha* to Makkos (24a).

Page 200 *Lev Eliyahu, Parashas Yisro,* p. 120.

Page 202 *Imrei Mordechai* (Rabbi Mordechai Shapiro), p. 142, fn.

Page 204 *Likutei Moharan,* Part II, 78:7.

Page 206 *Zemiroth*, by Rabbi Nosson Scherman, Mesorah Publications, p. 100.

Page 208 Rabbi Ettlinger's *Aruch LaNer* to *Succah* 41a.

Page 210 *Tzavaas HaBesht*; *Kesser Shem Tov* 220:1.

Page 212 *Ben Ish Chayil*, Vol. I, *Shabbos Zachor, Derush* 4.

Page 214 Rabbi Auerbach's *Minchas Shlomo,* Vol. I, 91:27.

This volume is part of

THE **ARTSCROLL**® SERIES

an ongoing project of

translations, commentaries and expositions on
Scripture, Mishnah, Talmud, Midrash, Halachah,
liturgy, history, the classic Rabbinic writings,
biographies and thought.

*For a brochure of current publications visit your local
Hebrew bookseller or contact the publisher:*

313 Regina Avenue • Rahway, New Jersey 07065
(718) 921-9000 • www.artscroll.com